Emerging Approaches to Law Firm Profitability

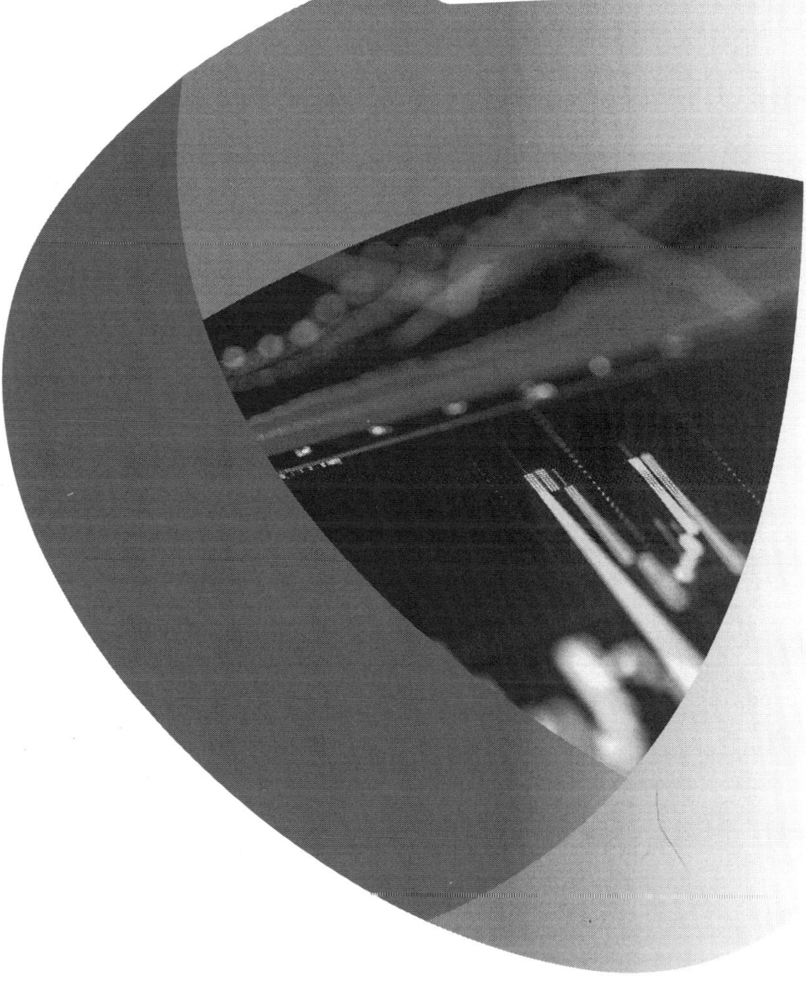

EDITED BY FRANCESCA RAMADAN

Head of events and books
Leah Darbyshire

Commissioning editor
Alex Davies

Editorial assistant
Francesca Ramadan

Published by ARK Group:

UK, Europe and Asia office
5th Floor
10 Whitechapel High Street
London, E1 8QS
United Kingdom
Tel: +44(0) 207 566 5792
publishing@ark-group.com

North America office
4408 N. Rockwood Drive, Suite 150
Peoria IL 61614
United States
Tel: +1 (309) 495 2853
publishingna@ark-group.com

www.ark-group.com

Printed by Canon (UK) Ltd, Cockshot Hill, Reigate, RH2 8BF, United Kingdom

ISBN: 978-1-78358-334-8

A catalogue record for this book is available from the British Library

ARK Group is a division of Wilmington plc. The company is registered in England & Wales with company number 2931372 GB. Registered office: 5th Floor, 10 Whitechapel High Street, London E1 8QS.

VAT Number: GB 899 3725 51.

Contents

Executive summary

The legal profession, like so many other fields, has continued to reel from the deep-reaching and significant impact of the 2008 financial crisis. In the years following the crash, a general downward turn in the demand for legal services compelled firms to tighten their belts, make tough decisions, and come up with innovative strategies in order to survive. One of these was an increased focus on profitability and different means of managing and improving it, a relatively new development for the legal industry. However, in recent years there have been small but positive signs of improvement, manifested in a gradual pick-up in client engagement, as global economies continue to slowly but steadily recover from the crash. It is definitely a better time to be a lawyer, as latent demand begins to manifest in parallel with growing client confidence in a stabilizing market, fast-paced disruptive technological innovations, and significant changes in laws and regulations.

However, this does not mean that firms can afford to be complacent. The legal landscape continues to be in flux, and improvement is slow. Increased revenue and client demand does not come to firms that do not proactively seek it, nor is it achieved by those who are not applying innovative and cutting-edge techniques and strategies to the management of their firm. Of course, delivering the best service to clients should always be a top priority; however, there should also be an emphasis on running the firm like a business, which includes intensive scrutiny of expenditure and coming up with new and inventive ways to generate profit. Managing and growing a firm's profitability should not just be an exercise for difficult economic periods, but instead must be a priority at all times. Rather than being perceived as an irksome bolt-on, it is necessary to see it as a great opportunity in these times of increased business.

Existing and persistent cultural norms amongst lawyers, however, means that the reform of current business practices does not always come naturally. Nor is it necessarily easy to find the right practical advice that can carry a firm through the transition. *Emerging Approaches to Law Firm Profitability* aims to be the ideal tool to assist with implementation, providing essential guidance for those seeking new means of maximizing their firm's capacity. Featuring advice and reflections from a wide variety of contributors, ranging from business and finance professionals to thought leaders and consultants, this book offers in-depth, intensive insight into the challenges generated by today's dynamic and hyper-competitive legal landscape. Most importantly, *Emerging Approaches to Law Firm Profitability* moves past the identification of these obstacles and supplies original, innovative ways of tackling them. Expert guidance is complemented by compelling case studies and effective real-world examples, supplying principles that can be applied to firms of any size or capacity.

It can be said that many of those working in law firms don't fully understand what drives their firm's revenue and how their everyday actions can have either a positive or negative impact. In chapter 1, Stuart Dodds of Positive Pricing seeks to provide a strong foundation on which to build and understand what really drives "the business of law". Themes covered include getting the basics right, the power of small changes, and challenging the status quo.

Taking into consideration the growing level of complexity and sophistication in the legal field, the days in which law firms operated in a profit paradise and could afford to eschew deep financial analysis are fading fast. In chapter 2, CEO of Advanced Financial Analytics and principal at Edge International, Ariela Tannenbaum, provides an overview of the methods by which firms can take a step forward and adopt a clear and concise financial lens, unlocking the management insight necessary to enhance performance. This insightful chapter will discuss topics such as the practice of disciplined financial review, attorneys' productivity measurements, and pricing optimization.

It is not enough to simply attempt to reform the way in which a law firm sees itself in order to boost profitability; an in-depth transformation of its mechanics and operational practices must also be performed. In chapter 3, Hélène Russell – author, trainer and consultant in knowledge management – highlights why continuous process improvement is no longer a "nice-to-have" and is in fact "table stakes" for many law firm clients. Strategic process design and improvement is defined, along with how it applies to law firms, and practical advice regarding where firms can start with their own process improvement pilot.

When it comes to optimizing profitability, the model used to measure it matters. In chapter 4, Peter Lane Secor – director of strategic pricing and project management at Pepper Hamilton LLP – undertakes a review of both fully loaded and cost-only profit methodologies, examining their pros and cons and delving into their relationship with partnership acceptance and its impact. This comprehensive analysis is designed to assist with a decision as to which method is best suited for a firm's culture.

Partners and firm directors and officers rely on profitability reports to make major decisions. As highlighted by the previous chapter, a proposed model is often subject to various criticisms, and the ability to gain acceptance ultimately determines its validity and the ability to use said model in those decisions. In chapter 5, Paige Keith – chief financial officer at Hawkins Parnell Thackston & Young LLP – examines proven tactics to design a profitability model that will stand up to cross-examination and provide a strong foundation for a successful profitability rollout.

Companies consistently face challenges and opportunities to enhance their business models and provide value to their customers, workforce, and owners. Not surprisingly, law firms are no different. Chapter 6, by Thomas W. Van Der Moere, chief financial officer at Neal, Gerber & Eisenburg, focuses on a firm's opportunity to scrutinize existing and potential business using client and product profitability analysis, shifting the focus away from billable hours and time-measured revenue and providing the insight that will allow a firm to direct its resources to areas where return can be maximized.

In a 2017 survey on law firm strategic planning (conducted by David J. Parnell and Patrick J. McKenna), it was found that – despite the perceived importance of law firm strategy and the heavy amounts of resources devoted to its creation – only 3.2 percent of responding firms implemented "almost all to all" of their strategy. While the need to develop a firmwide strategy is embraced by most firms, putting it into action is another matter altogether. Mobilizing boots on the ground requires highly detailed, individualized business plans that help the individual partner to truly understand their markets, resources, motivations, and place in the overall map. In chapter 7, David J. Parnell – columnist and founder and principal of True North Partner Management – will break down the partner-level business plan into its individual components, discuss them, and provide examples to help the reader better understand how this fits into the bigger picture.

In contrast to popular opinion, Srinivas Vadali – principal management consultant at PA Consulting – and Manish Khandelwal – IT transformation expert – state that it is insourcing, rather than outsourcing, that has been on the rise in recent years. As organizations become more agile and focused on their customer, insourcing enables them to re-balance their supply chains and keep critical skills in-house. In chapter 8, Srinivas and Manish offer their unique perspective and discuss practical steps on how companies can insource more services to boost profitability.

Traditionally, fee-earners have been measured on income and little else. However, in chapter 9, Rupert Hawke – managing director at UK firm Cartwright King – explains that it is important to understand why employees perform well as part of the larger, firm-wide revenue-generating strategy. A detailed model targeting the intersection between profitability and performance is delineated by Rupert, a helpful tool that will allow managers and fee-earners alike to see in simple form where performance is above or below expectation, why this might be, and what can be done to tackle it.

In the current climate, law firms are frequently encouraged to utilize innovative, technological solutions as a means of boosting profitability; in fact, factors such as the buzz at legaltech conferences mean that introducing technologies like AI and data analytics software is now seen as critical to a firm's success. However, in a saturated tech market which exists in a state of constant flux, it is often difficult for firm management to know where and how to begin. In chapter 10, Zev J. Eigen – founder and chief science officer of Syndio Solutions – offers his expertise as a data scientist to supply two readily available forms of innovation, which embrace the possibilities technology brings and provide creative and original ways of reframing profitability.

To conclude, chapter 11 – written by Katherine Thomas, consultant and former co-founder and director of Vario for Pinsent Masons – looks ahead to the future and explores the ways in which alternative approaches can support profitability and create a sustainable future for law firms. From flexible talent management to digital delivery, from automation to appropriate fee arrangements, Katherine looks at the opportunities that "newlaw" thinking presents. By combining the benefits of established law and newlaw, it is possible for firms to adapt to meet client needs profitably and more effectively.

About the authors

Stuart J T Dodds is co-founder and Principal of Positive Pricing, which provides pricing and legal project management strategy and implementation advice to the world's leading law firms. He was previously Baker McKenzie's director of global pricing and legal project management; prior to joining the firm, Stuart conducted a similar role at Linklaters, having previously worked as a management consultant for 17 years. He is an accredited Certified Pricing Professional (CPP), Accredited Legal Pricing Professional (ALPP), sits on a number of industry-related advisory bodies, and is a Fellow of the College of Law Practice Management.

Zev J. Eigen is the founder and chief science officer of Syndio, and a data scientist focused on AI and machine learning applications in HR, labor and employment law, and legal services broadly. He was honored as one of the *Financial Times*' 10 most innovative lawyers in 2016, as a FastCase50 Innovator of 2016, and as one of "40 Under 40 Rising Legal Stars" by the *National Law Journal*. He is frequently quoted in the media as an expert on big data solutions, predictive analytics and machine learning, especially as applied to HR and legal services and products.

Rupert Hawke is the managing director of the UK's Cartwright King Solicitors, having originally joined the firm as finance director in 2007. Holder of a business degree and a qualified management accountant, Rupert spent much of his career working for a large multi-national organisation before applying his wide-ranging experience and business acumen to the legal sector. He has overseen significant expansion at Cartwright King, which now has 19 offices nationwide, that he has contributed to with his development of management information systems and grasp of the modern business environment. Rupert is also the author of many articles advising on management within the legal sector.

Paige Keith is a business executive with extensive experience leading financial and accounting operations of law firms, including planning, reporting, billing, tax compliance, and accounts payable. Before becoming a chief financial officer at Hawkins Parnell Thackston & Young LLP, she spent 15 years in various management roles responsible for developing and implementing strategic initiatives. She has also overseen client relations and the delivery of legal services, emphasizing the design and integration of consumer-centric business models and technology. Paige studied at Southern Methodist University in Dallas, Texas, where she earned an MBA from the Cox School of Business and a BS in mechanical engineering with biomedical specialization.

Manish Khandelwal has an extensive range of management expertise and practical experience covering IT outsourcing, offshoring, procurement and business transformation. He has led various multi-million pound outsourcing and IT enabled change programs helping clients achieve the most from their sourcing and IT transformation initiatives. His areas of expertise include end-to-end management of outsourcing programs, procurement life-cycle management, contract management, supplier selection and management, change management, stakeholder management and relationship management. He has worked in delivery and pre-sales, led supplier sales teams and has a strong techno-commercial understanding of the offshoring business.

David J. Parnell is an author, speaker, *Forbes* and *American Lawyer Media* columnist, and the founder and principal of True North Partner Management, a partner-level legal search and placement firm. Along with his experience in private placement, he has previously worked in-house with the likes of Intel, Xircom, and DreamWorks SKG. Complimenting his *Forbes* and *ALM* columns, his work can also be found in publications such as *The American Lawyer*, *Huffington Post*, *Venture Capital Post*, *Fox News Magazine*, *Lawyerist*, *Law360*, *Bloomberg*, *Australasian Lawyer*, *NBC News*, *The Global Legal Post*, *Business Insider*, and *NZ Lawyer*, among others.

Hélène Russell of TheKnowledgeBusiness is a lawyer and specialist in knowledge management. After working in clinical negligence litigation defense work for eight years, followed by two years in an in-house KM team, she has been self-employed since 2008. Hélène specializes in distilling complex academic thought leadership and cross-boundary theories into practical tools to improve the efficiency and profitability of real-life law firms. As well as being an author of two practical textbooks, she also teaches open and in-house courses in knowledge management and offers coaching, mentoring, and advice.

Peter Lane Secor is the director of strategic pricing and project management with Pepper Hamilton LLP. Mr. Secor concentrates on legal project management, with focuses of improving efficiencies through shared management responsibilities, strengthening communication and making value transparent. Servicing law firms for almost 20 years, he has developed accurate methods for pricing, budgeting, forecasting, performance management analysis, and conveying client/matter profitability. These competencies enable him to design and manage creative fee arrangements which bring value to both Pepper and its clients. He has provided presentations for TVPi, ALA, LMA, ILTA, ABA, Law Vision, Buying Legal, ARK, Aderant and other organizations on both national and regional levels.

Ariela Tannenbaum is the CEO of Advanced Financial Analytics, a consultancy firm focusing on enhancing law firms' profitability, and principal at Edge International. She has over 25 years of top tier leadership experience working with global Fortune 500 companies, instilling the financial intelligence and discipline used by the most successful organizations in the world to drive performance at law firms. Prior to establishing Advanced Financial Analytics, Ms. Tannenbaum served as executive vice president of finance at one for the largest companies in the world and global head of finance of its $2 trillion investment management subsidiary for over 14 years.

Katherine Thomas helps legal service providers across the world grow, adapt and increase profitability with her company Katherine Thomas Consulting. With a reputation for strategic thinking combined with a large dose of pragmatism, she advises on strategy, sales, client development and the launch of new products and services. Now a consultant, speaker and coach, she previously established and led the well-known UK newlaw business Vario, a legal services provider with an emphasis on flexibility, for commercial law firm Pinsent Masons. As a result, she has a deep understanding of how alternative approaches to legal services delivery can increase competitiveness.

Srinivas Vadali is a seasoned consultant and C-suite advisor with more than 17 years of experience in shaping strategy and delivering major change and transformation programs. He has expertise in commercial services, sourcing, business case/financial management, transition and location strategy. The focus of Srini's work is to help clients improve the value delivered by their business services arrangements, establishing in-house and outsourced shared services and using technology to drive organizational change and improvement in business performance. His client base over the last 17 years has included wide range of financial services institutions, including a premier stock exchange, commercial insurance, retail and core banking.

Thomas Van Der Moere is the chief financial officer at Neal, Gerber & Eisenberg LLP, a Chicago-based law firm with over 140 lawyers, where he oversees the financial operations of the firm including the areas of accounting, treasury management, planning/analytics/business intelligence, practice economics and strategic pricing, financial systems, and new business acceptance and risk management. Tom has expertise in professional service firm administrative and financial management, performance and compensation analysis, financial and operational analysis and modeling, strategic planning, process development and re-engineering, firm/project profitability and risk management, and business intelligence. He also has significant financial experience with public and private companies in professional services, energy, and manufacturing industries. Tom has an MBA from the University of Chicago Booth School of Business and an MS in Accounting and Business Management from the University of Tulsa.

Chapter 1:
Law firm economics 101 – understanding the business of law

By Stuart J T Dodds, co-founder and principal of Positive Pricing

The focus on law firm profitability is as acute as ever – moving from a temporary area of focus to one of the top law firm management priorities. However, having "focus" is not the same as having a good "understanding" of what drives the business of law. Are we really aware of what factors influence how law firms make money and, as importantly, how not to *lose* money? Many firms still often focus on the potential revenue line, seldom paying attention to the expense to winning a piece of work from existing or (especially) new clients, or in mitigating "silly mistakes" which can impact profitability.

This chapter provides an overview to the key drivers of law firm profitability, some current (as of mid-2018) market context, and how the "status quo" is being challenged. An awareness and understanding of each of these drivers is vital to ensure that firms continue to price and perform client matters cost effectively whilst delivering the now-expected levels of client value and service.

But why does profitability matter? Apart from the obvious (compensation) element, strong profitability is critical in having a strong market profile, strong league table rankings, overall competitive positioning, lateral recruitment, attorney retention, and finally future investment (for example, office openings or major infrastructure projects). Achieving a competitive level of profitability is therefore rightly regarded as being fundamental to a firm's ability in sustaining its overall competitiveness. What is becoming apparent is that there's a critical need to *actively* manage profitability on a number of dimensions – at a firm, practice and individual level, by work type and by client – and, by their very nature, some of these themes are "macro" or "micro".

Making money

Let's start at the very beginning. How does a law firm make money?

The ability of a firm to deliver revenue is driven by the markets in which it operates (including current and potentially new clients), the nature of services it provides, and finally the relative value placed on these services by the client. A firm's ability to generate fees (or "fee capacity") is therefore a proportion or subset of the overall revenue potential. Fee capacity is linked to the number of timekeepers, their seniority and expertise; (historically) the number of hours they would expect to work for their clients; and the rate that they would typically conduct this work for. External factors also play a key role. The volume of matters conducted, the nature of these matters, and the competitive pricing pressure from other firms all play a role in either limiting this fee capacity potential or increasing it.

What this traditional approach reinforces is the view that revenue is based on hours worked for the client, rather than the fundamental tenet of pricing, i.e. that the price should reflect the appropriate value to the client rather than the cost of production cost (i.e. hours worked). It therefore places a false limit on the potential fee capacity for those partners and law firms willing to be more flexible in the fee approaches adopted and level of risk shared with their clients (for example, through pricing on a contingent of fixed fee basis).

The basics of law firm profitability

For the past decade, most law firms have experienced a "twin squeeze" on their profitability – declining or relatively static revenue coupled with the need to manage expenses. The resultant "gap" between the two, the revenue *not* expended, being "profit".

Happily, we seem to be at least witnessing some growth, albeit modest. As an example, growth across the top 100 US firms was greater in 2017 than any time since the global financial crisis, with revenues rising by 5.5 percent.[1] UK law firm financial figures reported have also been similarly positive, with growth between two and four percent.[2] Although good news, this rise has not necessarily been matched everywhere with significant variations by firm. The hard work is clearly not quite over, especially if one considers that the top three firms account for 10 percent of the AM Law 100 revenues, and 25 percent from the top nine (the same proportion as the bottom 50!).[3]

The first theme – that of declining or relatively static revenue – continues to be driven by the downward pressure on fees. This can be very significant as new entrants seek to aggressively price to take market share, coupled with a reduction in certain types of work and increasing influence of client legal operations and procurement teams.

The second theme – managing expenses – is being impacted by the upward pressure on direct costs and an increase in investment, especially with IT and AI.[4] Costs are also rising due to the ongoing competition for the "best" laterals in the market (especially acute in the UK driven by US firm hiring strategies), driving associated compensation costs higher in the hope that these "stars" bring in significant additional revenues once in situ. The last 12 months have also seen an increase in associate compensation in many US-based firms, resulting in higher direct expenses despite the fact that the rise in indirect costs is slowing. Overall recent data indicates that expenses are running about 3–5 percent higher year on year as of 2016.[5]

Watching the revenue line

If growth really is at best limited one response is to focus on and conduct better and smarter management of the revenue line itself. In a law firm, and indeed other professional service firms which sell expertise rather than a product, revenue is impacted by four key drivers:

- The rate the firm is able to charge their clients;
- Overall realization;
- Their productivity; and
- The number of lawyers present (and how well they are used).

Let's take each in turn:

1. Rates

Of the four key drivers, this is probably best understood. Until the global financial crisis, law firms were typically able to increase their standard rates by anywhere between six and 10 percent per annum (depending upon jurisdiction). Given that underlying costs were rising at significantly more modest level (between two and four percent depending upon jurisdiction), the resulting difference between these two numbers was pure profit. It was this difference which drove the rapid increase in many firms' level of partner profit, and which has perhaps set the unrealistic compensation expectations today as partners compare current levels of profit to the "golden days" pre-2008 (although some firms are continuing to thrive).

The world changed. Many law firms are now lucky if they can achieve a more modest 3-4 percent increase in rates through to their clients (the average rate increase of the AM Law 100 in 2017 was estimated to be 3.1 percent[6]). Coupled with similar, if not higher, level of costs, the current level of rate increases at best keep many firms cost- and revenue-neutral, with rising rates merely compensating for rising costs. With many clients, particularly since late 2008, instituting "rates freezes" for two or sometimes three years based on pure math alone, unless a law firm proactively seeks to move away from hourly based billing *and* also improve their overall efficiency, they will experience declining profitability from these clients year on year. It is therefore apparent that increasing rates is no longer a viable solution in trying to address, or at least mask, the more inherent challenges within the legal industry.

2. Realization

The second key driver is realization, which can be defined a number of ways. The most commonly used definition is this being the percentage of the firm's standard billing rate actually collected. It is a metric which converts the "time value" into cash receipts (with "time value" being the product of demand – i.e. billable hours, and pricing – i.e. hourly rates). Realization is impacted by three main factors, reflecting:

- Any agreed upon discounts given to a client;
- Any "write-downs", which are reductions made to the bill *before* sending; and
- Any "write-offs", which are reductions made *after* the bill has been sent.

Although it is very much an internal measure, monitoring realization is vital to any law firm for one reason above all others. It is what I call the "1 – 3 – 4 rule" which basically states that a one percent increase in realization can drive approximately a three percent improvement in profitability (depending upon the underlying cost base, and assuming a 35 percent firm-wide average profit margin). However, the converse is also true!

As a metric, it is commonly looked at a matter level, client level and firm-wide level. However, the metric, if viewed in isolation, can be misleading. Take the following two scenarios. Firm A achieves very high realization but has done so due to very low rates. In this example, Firm A has potentially left some money on the table. Firm B on the other hand, has relatively low realization, but against higher rates. They have done so intentionally based on their pricing and discounting policy. Firm B has lower realization but higher overall revenue. Unless you understand what is driving realization, you may come to an incorrect conclusion about how your firm, practice group or client team are performing.

Challenging the status quo – part one

It is also useful to examine realization at its component level. Although the usual definition of realization is the percentage of the firm's standard billing rate actually collected, there are a number of other approaches which can be as, and often more, useful. An article by James Cotterman (published in 2012) expanded upon this in a bit more detail.[7] In the article, James argues that it is important to understand more fully the various components of realization, and how these impact realization. There are seven components, outlined below:

1. Where a timekeeper discounts their time at point of timesheet entry (either intentionally or otherwise) impacting potential revenue capture;
2. Write downs of unbilled time (most common);
3. Client adjustments which result in write-offs to receivables, through more active client monitoring of billing;
4. Pricing variance. Although firms typically measure realization against the respective timekeeper's standard (rack) rate, this can also be done against their agreed client rate (if, for example, discounts are given). The variance can be a useful measure to determine how effective the discounting approach has been. Whereas standard rate realization reflects not only the impact of any pricing decisions, but also the impact of matter management, staffing, and service efficiency, actual rate realization removes the pricing element, allowing more granular analysis;
5. Efficiency variance, which looks at the non-pricing issues which impact realization, such as staffing decisions and overall process efficiency. Another part of this component is the "speed of collections", with slower collections and/or longer billing cycles leading to less money being collected, lower realization and also higher working capital requirements;
6. Turnover of unbilled time. In other words, what has been worked but not yet billed. For most firms this is typically between 1.5 and 2.5 months; and
7. Turnover of accounts receivable (AR). In other words, how many months of revenue are sitting in fees receivable. This is also typically between 1.5 and 2.5 months (for most), which in turn impacts a firm's working capital requirements.

Therefore, if just looking at realization through the more traditional lens, we would not be able to identify, and therefore appropriately address, some of the underlying root causes of potentially poor performance. As the article concludes, "(t)he appropriate remedy will vary based on the cause… (and)…(t) he only way to get to the cause is to get into the details." [(8)]. To make realization as a metric meaningful – that is exactly what we need to do.

3. Productivity matters?

Our third lever is productivity (or "utilization"); this is defined as the total number of billable hours recorded, divided by the number of lawyers at a law firm. It is a key indicator of how successful a firm is using their available fee earning resources, and underlying demand for their services. As context, when looking at the United States for 2017, productivity was down slightly on the previous year at around 0.6 percent, driven by two key factors: relatively static demand coupled with the number of lawyers joining the profession, estimated by some at around 1.5 percent in 2017.[9] However, assessing "success" based on the actual costs of production (the "inputs", most commonly billable hours), rather than in the value we are generating for our clients (the "outputs"), is flawed. Getting better at pricing and aligning that price to the value important to the client is more critical.

4. The magic ingredient: leverage

The fourth and final driver is "leverage" (sometimes referred to as "gearing"). It is *the* magic ingredient to better profitability and is a key focus of our clients as they seek better value for money. This means pushing work down to the lowest appropriate level to do the work efficiently, which may mean a partner in some instances.

It is the amount of non-equity partner work done per equity partner, often expressed in the form "1: <number>". For example, if leverage was shown as being "1:5", this would indicate one equity partner hour worked for each five hours of non-equity partner time work (regardless of level). It is this metric which is the most powerful lever in improving profit.

Taking this concept to the logical extreme, this then drives better resourcing at a lower overall cost (i.e. lower client fees) and improves the overall profitability of the matter for the law firm. Very seldom in life do two mutually desired objectives present themselves in one simple solution. *Better leverage* is that solution. It is also one that law firms can directly control and is not dependent upon market forces. If only for this reason alone, law firms should embrace the basics of legal project management and, perhaps more pertinently here, legal process improvement.

Profitability: a meaningful measure?

Most law firms have wrestled with how best to express their respective profitability in a meaningful way. Some have used measures based on the effective financial contribution per partner hour (more on this later), others having more or less sophisticated metrics. Coupled with this, there are a myriad of ways to allocate cost, each based on firm preference (or ignorance of other methods).

Profitability is driven by the allocation of direct and indirect expenses to the firm. This is done for each matter (as appropriate) with these costs then being deducted from the matter fees received. At the aggregate, firm-wide level, this then is divided across all equity partners to give an average, the (in)famous PEP, or "profit per equity partner" (some also known as PPP, "profit per partner"). This has become the key reporting metric for most law firms, giving those with higher PEP bragging rights in the lawyer playground in the pages of *The American Lawyer* (who were instrumental in developing the metric, and promotion of its usage years ago through its annual league tables, since adopted in other jurisdictions).

However, fundamental issues with the actual PEP/PPP metric itself remain. It can drive short-term behavior in a pursuit of immediate revenue. It ignores a range of other determinants of law firm "health" such as client retention, client satisfaction, law firm retention and morale and, indeed, firm-wide profitability. It does not account for any pro-bono or CSR initiatives undertaken by a firm. And most crucially, it does not attempt to reflect the "value" the law firm has (hopefully) added for their clients.

Its method of calculation is also open to interpretation. It is determined by the average of firm-wide profit divided by all equity partners, yet a number of articles focused on law firm profitability note that the equity spread from the highest to lowest earning partners in some firms may be as high as nine to one throughout the AM Law 100. It is self-reported by firms themselves, each providing details of firm revenue, profit and number of "eligible" partners – this in turn leading to a broader question around how it is calculated and whether it really is a like-for-like comparison.

However, it gives a focus. Although there is not necessarily anything better on the immediate horizon, we would be well served to recognize the dangers of slavishly adhering the mantra of PEP/PPP while the search for a more meaningful metric continues. The challenge of any profitability metric is that it can become divisive unless properly understood. It is also critical to view profitability in the longer (or at least mid) term. Looking at profitability on a specific matter may be helpful as means to redirect a matter veering off its intended course, but much greater value can be looking at this measure at a client or practice area/ service level to see how this compares against the relative peer group.

Challenging the status quo – part two

A number of commentators, and indeed firms, are beginning to challenge the more traditional profitability metrics. In an article for *The American Lawyer* in July 2017,[10] Hugh Simons proposed the adoption of using "margin per partner hour" (MPH) to more appropriately measure profitability against measures which were in partner's control and which encouraged them to take (if necessary) corrective action.

In summary, this metric "enables assessment of profitability on matters with widely varying realisation and leverage in a directly comparable way."[11] It recognizes firstly what is directly in the partner's control (namely, the amount of realized revenue and staffing/time expended on the matter) and also measures effective use of scare resource (i.e. partner time), resulting in a more appropriate metric looking at margin on a per partner hour expended basis. As Hugh summarizes "MPH is in essence the matter-level counterpart of the summary PPP/PEP metric".[12] A number of law firms have adopted this type of metric for a while, at least one having in place for nearly a decade a metric of "contribution per partner hour" (CPPH).

The value of this type of metric is significant. It is less concerned with a timekeeper's *overall* utilization within the law firm (only focusing on time on the matter) and resultant compensation and cost, although each certainly plays a part in wider firm profitability metrics. It also allows more efficient and effective comparisons across similar matters (with the MPH measure being more appropriate for the work at hand – for example, the MPH on tax work would be very different from IP work and so on); enable pricing discussions to be more action-orientated (encouraging greater discussion on appropriate client investments and staffing); and also support more proactive support to those partners who are experiencing lower than expected margin (for example, pricing, negotiation or legal project management support).

It is not the "silver bullet", however, as limitations do exist. One is the acknowledgement of how partner time is measured, and more specifically cost allocated, and impact on resultant profitability. It also assumes that partners are able to spend their time on other potential revenue-generating opportunities when not spending time on the matter. However, it should be an integral part of the profitability metric mix.

Conclusion

We are now reaching a point where profitability is best viewed at a more aggregate and comprehensive level rather than via a single metric, allowing more informed decisions to be taken – not only at an immediate pricing level, but also in how these matters are being managed and staffed.

It perhaps goes without saying that law firms need to make sure their partners and senior professional staff are aware of what drives law firm profitability. Many don't. They also need to make sure all understand what these various metrics mean and how they work in tandem.

If used well, these measures should help drive the pursuit of the "right revenue". Not just any revenue, but revenue which delivers an appropriate level of profit to the law firm at an acceptable cost to the client (when aligned to the value being delivered). However, these metrics do need interpretation. This in turn requires a different and complementary skill than that possessed by a large number of lawyers: financial analysis. So, step forward those in finance, business management and (increasingly) pricing roles – become the business advisors you have always wanted to be.

References

1. *The American Lawyer*, The 2018 AM Law 100 Rankings (The American Lawyer, 24 April 2018).
2. Citi Client Advisory, *2018: Client Advisory: The Legal Market in 2017* (Citi Private Bank/ Hildebrandt Consulting, December 2017), 4.
3. Bruce MacEwen, Thomson Reuters Forum, *But What Do The AM Law Numbers Really Show?* (Thomson Reuters Forum, September 2017), vol 3, ed 2, 36–37.
4. Thomson Reuters Peer Monitor/ Georgetown Law Center for the Study of the Legal Profession, *2018: Report on the State of the Legal Market* (Thomson Reuters, February 2018), 3.
5. *Ibid.*, 9.
6. *Ibid.*, 6.
7. James D. Cotterman, *Issues in Realization* (Altman Weil, 2012)
8. *Ibid.*, 6
9. Citi Client Advisory, *2018: Client Advisory: The Legal Market in 2017* (Citi Private Bank/ Hildebrandt Consulting, December 2017), 3.
10. Hugh A. Simons, *How Firms Should Be Measuring the Profitability of Matters* (The American Lawyer, 28 July 2017).
11. *Ibid.*
12. *Ibid.*

Sources

Parts of this chapter previously appeared in the author's book, *Smarter Pricing, Smarter Profit* (American Bar Association, May 2014).

Chapter 2:
Accounts receivable, billable hours, and collections: the end game or a starting point?

By Ariela Tannenbaum, CEO of Advanced of Financial Analytics and principal at Edge International

When it comes to financial performance, most small to mid-size law firms focus on their ABCs: accounts receivable (keep 'em low!), billable hours (keep 'em high!), and collections (100 percent would be nice!). But true financial intelligence – and the success that flows from it – requires more. It is not enough for firms to zero-in on a snapshot of these three predominant measurements of financial success because, while important, they only tell part of the story.

Imagine yourself driving a car, but only able to see what appears in your rearview mirror: no forward view of the road beyond, no speedometer, tachometer, gas gauge, navigation system, compass, thermometer, park assist... you get the picture. You might have a pretty clear sense of where you've been, but where you are headed and the hazards that lie up the road are anybody's guess. Likewise, a law firm may have a highly-competent bookkeeper, accountant, controller, or even a chief financial officer to serve the essential role of digesting reams of accounting data and presenting a picture of the firm's past financial performance to leadership.

But what is too often lacking is true "financial intelligence" – a forward-thinking, strategic plan that goes beyond the "What have we billed? What have we collected? What are we owed?" paradigm that inevitably leaves you one step behind. What is "financial intelligence"? It is a powerful tool your C-level colleagues in the corporate realm have long utilized to maximize profits. Fortune 500 companies have long-relied on sophisticated financial tools to chart their financial success, and those same tools can be scaled and applied to law firms. These tools allow a law firm to:

- Convert accounting data into management insight;
- Accurately project future financial performance;

- Dive into financial health and profitability trends by practice area, office, client, and industry;
- Identify profitability levers;
- Gain clear visibility into the firm's strengths and weaknesses; and
- Develop concrete plans to enhance profitability.

But before you can put these tools to use, you must stop seeing the law firm as a *practice* and start running it as a *business* – a profit-driven entity with a forward-looking vision and a realistic, operative plan for success. Consider whether you can answer the following questions in confident detail:

1. What is the profit margin of the firm?
2. What is the profitability of each one of the practice areas?
3. What has been the profitability trend by practice area over the last three years?
4. What is the projected profitability?
5. Do you have an actionable plan to "fix" the weaker practice areas and enhance the stronger ones?
6. How do you optimize pricing in response to the increasing demand for alternative fee arrangements?
7. What is the revenue loss associated with discounted billing hours and rates? Is there an upward or downward trend?
8. What is the profitability of top ten clients?
9. How will a potential departure of a partner impact bottom-line profitability?
10. What is your firm's financial outlook for the next six to 12 months?

A managing partner who cannot answer these questions will never break out of the all-too-common cycle of perpetually playing Monday-morning quarterback.

So how do you arm yourself with the data needed to answer these and other key questions and finally break out of the backward-looking cycle once and for all? You employ the corporate world's sophisticated financial tools to convert your accounting data and trends into management insight. This will allow you to concisely identify the direction your firm is heading, its strengths and shortcomings, risks, and opportunities so that you can consciously and purposefully act to increase profitability.

To truly run your firm as a profit-maximizing business, you must have a pragmatic yet holistic overview of the firm's operations, and be thoroughly informed of all performance indicators at all times – so that you can take prompt, decisive action to stay on course to meet your financial objectives. This requires a multi-step process.

The budget

As a starting point, it is imperative that a firm develop an annual financial budget that mirrors its strategic plans. Mission statements, vision declarations, and strategic plans have little value unless they are accompanied by a measuring mechanism. The budget creates a sense of commitment and a measurable indicator for the leadership of the firm. For the budget to be effective, it needs buy-in from all stakeholders, and an all-hands budget development process is therefore ideal.

The regular financial review

While the budget is a critical starting point, it is not enough. Firm management needs a disciplined monthly or quarterly financial review, which should include the following topics:

- A clear picture of the firm's financial health – year-to-date P&L results;
- Precise financial projections and reasons for any variance from the budget;
- Revenue, profitability, and profit margin by major drivers – attorney, practice area, industry, client, and office;
- Revenue analysis – hourly and alternative fees;
- Expense analysis including expense drivers;
- Profitability and profit margin per (significant) matter;
- Productivity drivers and trends by attorney, practice area, office and firm-wide;
- Impact of potential upside/downside on profitability;
- Profitability levers;
- Impact of changes in hours and fee rates on revenue; and
- Benchmarking.

The monthly or quarterly financial review should ideally be in person and include the senior leadership of the firm and a finance professional. The discipline of a formal, in-person meeting and discussion of the financial review provides the firm management a platform to best realize and discuss the financial impact of the operational strategies and adjust as needed. It empowers management to make decisions with conviction and it is a pre-emptive approach proven to mitigate risks and stabilize the firm's bottom-line.

Look back or look ahead? Differentiate between lagging and leading indicators

While a law firm can and should be run like a business, you can never lose sight of the type of business it is and the unique dynamics that influence financial success. For example: measuring attorney billable hours and total revenue production is important for last year's productivity. But to optimize future productivity, one must look at the "intersection" of utilization rate by attorney and realization rate. The future earnings of the firm depend largely upon the attorneys with highest utilization *and* realization rates.

But first, what do "utilization" and "realization" mean in this context? Both utilization and realization rates are key performance indicators in measuring productivity in law firms: utilization measures the efficiency of attorney time. The utilization rate simply measures the time an attorney spends on serving a client versus the time the client is billed – for example, an attorney spends 100 hours on a client matter but bills only 80 hours; his or her utilization rate therefore is 80 percent on this matter.

The realization rate refers to the difference between the standard billing rate and the actual fee paid by the client. For example, an attorney's hourly billing rate is $500 but the collected fee is $450 per hour. The realization rate is $450/$500 or 90 percent. Clearly, looking at utilization and realization on an annual basis can provide a clear picture of the productivity level at the firm.

Some attorneys bill a large number of hours, but perhaps at lower hourly rates or at low collection rates. Others may have high hourly and collection rates, but lower gross billable hours. Understanding and measuring the intersection between these factors tells you which lawyers in your firm are contributing most to your bottom line. True financial intelligence provides this information to firm management in an easily digestible graphic format.

By way of example:

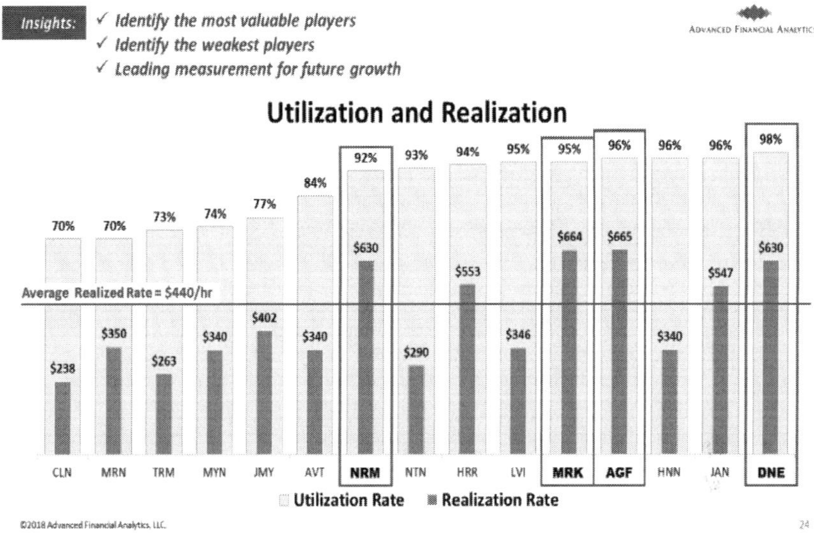

One billable hour with the highest utilization and realization rates results in more value to the firm than multiple billable hours with low utilization and realization rates. In fact, the latter hours are a drain on the firm's resources. Clearly, it is in the firm's best interest to maximize the number of billable hours that shine in both measures. To this end, proper coaching, mentoring, and promoting those individuals – and training others to emulate them – will drive up profits.

Understand and optimize pricing

In the context of optimizing performances and enhancing the bottom line, the analysis must include a consideration of pricing.

As an example, take fixed fee pricing. In a recent conversation with a senior partner of a well-reputed firm, when I asked about how his firm set a fixed fee for any given client matter, the partner shrugged his shoulders and remarked casually, "I come up with a number. It is a 'go' or 'no go' depending almost entirely on the client budget."

That is one way of going about it, of course, but as fee pressure increases, the "casual" method becomes less advantageous, especially for large matters. It becomes imperative to optimally price matters: high enough to be profitable and low enough to be competitive.

One approach is to estimate the number of hours involved and identify the corresponding compensation cost. To properly compute the compensation cost, it is important to assign a certain level of compensation per partner. As a benchmark, consider the base compensation of an executive at similar size corporation. The second level of cost is associated with overhead allocation. The third level of cost to be considered is harder to measure precisely; it is the cost of the risk of unknown complication(s) that might arise. Lastly, a profit margin should be applied. When computing a fee in this fashion, the firm can easily quantify their minimum fee, the "glass floor".

The "glass floor" should never fall below the compensation cost and must cover a certain percent of the overhead cost. When examining pricing from this angle, a firm's ability to offer competitive yet profitable pricing crystalizes.

Additionally, to mitigate risk, one ought to communicate pricing effectively with the client and precisely describe all elements included in the quoted price (i.e., the anticipated number of depositions, anticipated hours involved in drafting an agreement) but also include a "collar".

The collar sets a more specific ceiling and floor to the price. For example, a 20 percent collar means that if the cost associated with the matter is 20 percent over the quoted price, the client has to pay the cost over the 20 percent at a (potentially) discounted rate. If the cost is lower than anticipated and drops below 80 percent of the quoted price, the client is rewarded the difference.

While this particular illustration addresses fixed fees, this same pricing approach should apply to all matters, from traditional hourly to full contingency arrangements. While the analysis may change slightly, the fundamental variables – compensation cost, overhead allocation, risk, and profit margin – are the same.

Beware of "analysis paralysis"

While I strongly agree with legendary business guru Peter Drucker that "what gets measured, gets improved," one must be careful so to not drown in too much analysis. The term "analysis paralysis" stems from reality. Make sure to measure only what is most relevant to your firm. An analysis of hourly rate pricing is of little value to a firm that handles cases solely on a contingency basis, and vice versa.

Change is hard, but it's worth it

The growing level of complexity and the sophistication in the legal field, coupled with all external forces acting on it – rising competitive pricing, increase in demand for alternative fees arrangements with imbedded financial risks, decreases in realization rates, a rise in alternative service providers, and the shifting of work to in-house legal departments – are presenting a significant challenge to the legal field. The days in which law firms operated in a profit paradise and could afford to eschew deep financial analysis are fading fast.

As law firms have come to realize the uphill battle to preserve margins and enhance profits, they have enriched their talent pool with marketing and technology professionals. But too many law firms still leave money on the table, although they don't know they do and certainly don't know how much. I do bear some good news: lawyers do not need to work any harder or smarter, but they need to view themselves as a business and run their practice like the successful corporations they represent. It is time to take another step forward and see the firm though the clear and concise financial lens, unlocking the management insight you deserve to enhance your firm's performances.

Of course, change is hard. Moving beyond the ABCs to a true holistic picture of a firm's finances, a sharp and deep X-ray like picture, can sometimes spark delicate and potentially explosive intra-firm politics and a diversion from its objective. It is prudent to have a third-party, consultant approach the analysis with a truly objective outlook, fresh corporate-world perspective. The resulting analysis should present to you a measured assessment of the firm's present state, financial impact of operational strategies, a detailed plan of how to reach its financial objectives, and a clear path to maximize profits.

Chapter 3: Better, faster, cheaper – why clients expect law firms to know about process improvement

By Hélène Russell, founder of TheKnowledgeBusiness

I recently came across an exchange on LinkedIn about the use of checklists by conveyancing lawyers. Interestingly, most lawyers had expressed a negative opinion. I was surprised to see comments suggesting that checklists were just for junior lawyers, that checklists had no place in complex work, and even that clients wouldn't choose to instruct lawyers whom they knew used checklists.

I may be naïve, but I was genuinely surprised by these comments. The divergence between these comments on the value of knowledge management (the "know-how" aspect of knowledge management, at least) and those of the law firm leaders I had met earlier that week at Lexpo 2018 was particularly stark. The use of checklists is well-established to support complex surgery and aviation, so it was a surprise to see lawyers considering their conveyancing work too complex for even this straightforward and accessible type of process improvement.

It may soon be impossible for lawyers to ignore simple process improvements. There is a sense amongst General Counsel that costs have spiraled too far, which is echoed in the courts system. The recent Legal Services Board report found, from a sample base of 10,579 UK SMEs, only 11 percent of them believed that lawyers are a "cost effective means to resolve legal issues".[1]

For the moment, process design, management and improvement offer a competitive advantage to those firms which embrace it, but soon it may be a necessary part of practice management for even adequate profitability levels in law firms. Those firms which fail to embrace the opportunity now will struggle with the coming cultural changes.

This chapter therefore looks at why process design, management and improvement is a positive force: for individual lawyers, law firms as a whole, and clients.

What is process design and improvement?

"Processes" are all around. Making a cake or a cup of tea are both processes: a series of inputs (butter, sugar, flour, eggs, air, heat, jam, etc. or tea, water, milk and sugar) are applied to a process (the recipe) to turn them into an output.[2] How you get ready for work in the morning is probably a process you have streamlined over the years.

"Process design" in the legal sector is the designing of a legal service to make the activities of the processes involved in delivering that service more streamlined and coordinated. The purpose of process design is to meet the needs of clients more accurately through a balance of levels of quality, speed, dependability, flexibility and cost.

"Process mapping" is the visual depiction of existing processes within organizations in order to understand them and improve them ("process improvement").

Several different process improvement methodologies have emerged since 1980s, Lean and Six Sigma being the most well-known approaches. Although most process improvement methodologies emerged in manufacturing, they have been adapted and applied to service industries. Seyfarth Shaw LLP are probably the most well-known proponents of Lean Six Sigma (a tailored approach combining the most applicable aspects of Lean and Six Sigma), introducing it in response to client demand over a decade ago.

The benefits of process design, process improvement projects and continuous quality improvement systems

Process mapping helps identify improvements, such as:

- Eliminating unnecessary tasks (waste);
- Clarifying roles within the process and ensuring the right people undertake the right tasks;
- Reducing delays and duplication;
- Levels of "elapsed" and "effort" time; and
- Reducing the number of staff required within the process, freeing them for other work.

For clients, process design, management and improvement projects give them greater confidence in a firm's efficiencies, leading to greater transparency and enhanced relationships. It supports greater predictability, improved risk management and more accurate costs forecasting.

For law firms, for the reasons listed above, process improvements lead to more satisfied clients who dispute bills less often (being more confident of lack of wasted time)[3] and may also reduce debtor-days. The efficiency gains improve profits on fixed fees and enable competitive pricing on traditional time-based pricing. Process improvement projects currently enable smaller firms to differentiate themselves, although this will lessen as more firms use these techniques. Lastly, these projects improve quality through reducing duplication of work, delegating work to the right fee earner, freeing fee earners from non-chargeable work to focus on high value work, and identifying good and risky practices, affording the opportunity to minimize professional negligence claims.

For individual lawyers, process improvements enable good practice to be shared, reduce administrative tasks and free time for more complex, satisfying and high value work. They reduce non-chargeable work and write-offs, helping individuals to meet chargeable hour and billing targets. They also offer career development opportunities and transferable skills.

Those LinkedIn lawyers were concerned that checklists (one of the first varieties of process standardization) were too simplistic for their complex work. In fact, the removal of the need to remember and deal with simple administrative tasks actually frees mental space for tasks requiring higher brain function. There is also no need for processes to be limiting. Processes can be created or adapted for both complex and volume work. The best process management is flexible to meet the needs of the service to the client.

Where to start with your first process-related project

Beginning a process management initiative may seem daunting but there is no need to become Sayfarth Shaw overnight. Start making changes to small, short or simple processes in order to gain experience, and then begin to roll the methodology out more widely.

The following may be suitable for a first process analysis and improvement project:

- File opening procedures, conflict and money laundering checks;
- Billing procedures;
- Preparation of tenders;
- Preparation of e-newsletters; and
- Checking and sending of recurring reports to clients.

Alternatively, there may be an area, such as regular reporting on financial information or KPIs where your clients have suggested improvements, or an area suitable for standardized volume work where clients are looking for new, more competitively-priced suppliers.

Process analysis, management and improvement needn't require expensive technologies. Although there are technologies which can help map processes, the most important feature of these projects is the act of studying the process, finding and disseminating good practice, reducing duplication and waste, and delegating work to the most appropriate fee earner.

The best way to study the process is by drawing out a map of the inputs, outputs and activities. This can be done using specialist software but can also be easily mapped with a pen and paper or whiteboard and Post-It notes.

The biggest investment these projects require is that of time. Although you won't need an external consultant straightaway or to train your staff as Six Sigma blackbelts from the outset, it is likely that someone will need specialist training eventually and fee earner time will be needed both in the process mapping phase and the improvement phase.

There is no need to slavishly follow a methodology for your firm's first process improvement project, but you might find it simpler to draw on the DMAIC method from Six Sigma:

- **Define** the problem and why it needs to be solved;
- **Measure** the current performance of the process using a process map and any relevant business intelligence data which is available;
- **Analyze** the opportunities to reduce waste or variations;
- **Improve** the process by piloting, implementing and validating process changes; and
- **Control** the process to ensure sustained improvements.

Fee earners and support staff are usually pretty forthcoming about problems they have identified in everyday working life. Most people have noticed obviously wasteful processes. Alternatively, if there are difficulties in one field of practice which aren't easily articulated, root cause analysis tools[4] can help to identify a process which isn't working.

Stage 1 – map the process

Before putting pen to paper/fingers to keyboard, firstly gather evidence about what is occurring in the process under analysis. In order to gather the best evidence about the process, step back and have some quality discussions with those who are:

- Those who do the work;
- The suppliers to the process;
- The customers of the process (who could be internal or external); and
- The supervisors of the process.

Most people are happy to help with improvements to processes where mundane administration is stripped out, freeing them for more complex and interesting work. Fee earners in particular will be delighted if unnecessary non-chargeable work is removed, freeing them for more chargeable/billable work.

Stage 2 – Constructing the process map

When drawing out the process map, draw what is actually happening and do not muddle things with any ideas about what ought to be happening. If an existing process isn't being followed, look at the informal process and understand why it is preferred over the formal process and what is gained/lost as a result.

The symbols commonly used in process maps are set out below.

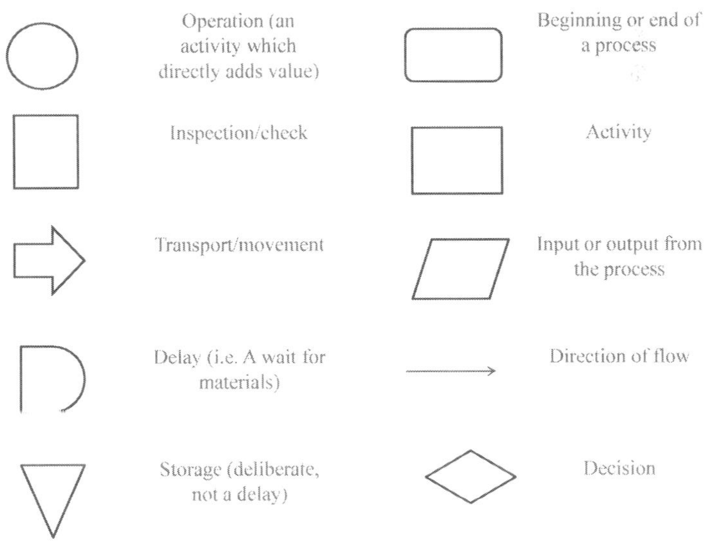

Figure 1: Common process map symbols

The symbols are arranged in order, in series and in parallel, to describe the process.

This can be done in a broad outline way, or at a more detailed level.[5]

A cross-functional element can be added to a simple flow chart, creating a "swim lane" diagram, which gives a clear visual representation of how the process flows through different departments and involves different people. This can be useful to understand how a draft bill flows between the hands of fee earners, administrators and cashiers before being sent to a client, for example.

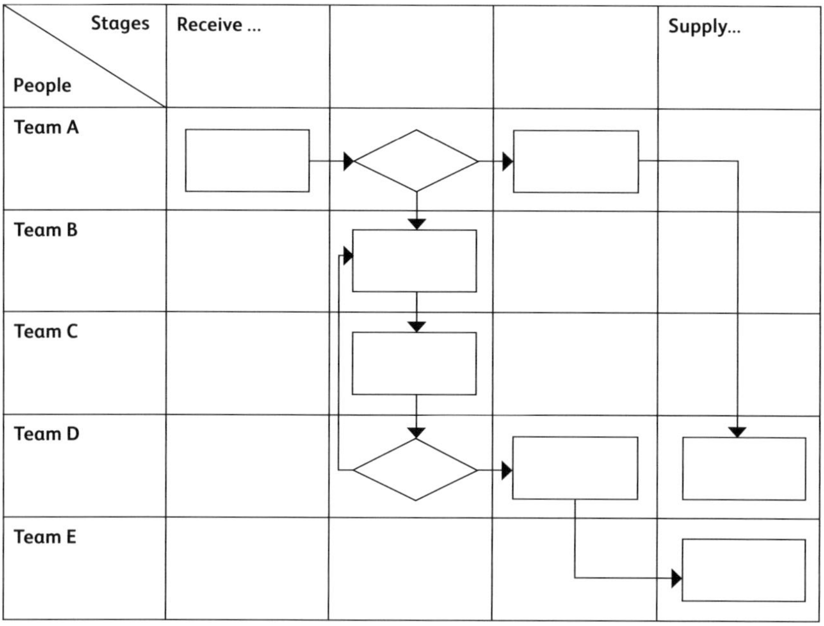

Figure 2: Example "swim lanes" diagram

Stage 2 – Analysis, critique and improvements

Often improvements to the process will become obvious as soon as the process is mapped out: they "leap off the page". Many inefficiencies creep in when small changes are made to a process over time without thought being given to the process as a whole. Sometimes a knee-jerk reaction to a problem adds a layer of supervision and checking which either isn't needed or is added at the wrong point in the process. By mapping the whole process, these inefficiencies and duplications become clear.

If improvements are not immediately obvious, the following questioning pattern is useful:

1. Why are we doing this? Why do we do it *this* way?
2. Is it essential to do this? Is it essential to do it *this* way?

Root cause analysis techniques, such as "5 whys" and "Fishbone/ Ishikawa diagrams" (see Appendix 4), can help to get to the heart of why a process is a certain way.

Ask:

- The implication of not doing parts of the process;
- The impact of change on internal and external customers/ stakeholders;
- Why the old process was thought to be necessary;
- What should be changed and why; and
- What the requirements are of the new process.

Consider also:

- Is there any re-work? Why are tasks not right the first time?
- Are there any completely unnecessary forms/paperwork/reports?
- Do people have access to the right equipment, and do they work from reliable and accurate information?
- Time
  - Are there any "bottlenecks" or areas where there is excessive delay? Are there areas where information is awaited?
  - Is any work being completed a long time before it is needed, and if so why? Does this cause problems with billing?
- Are all authorizations and supervision steps necessary?
- Are matters being dealt with by the right expert at the right level?

Use the answers to these questions to design the new process.

When the new process appears to be finished, ask:

- Have appropriate tasks been combined?
- Are decisions being made at the lowest appropriate level?
- Do the new steps in the process follow a natural order?

- Is the work being performed where and when it makes sense, by the right people and not by too many people?
- Are any backward movements and activities at the lowest level possible?

Stage 3 – Pilot changes and implement

How can a firm encourage lawyers, such as those opposing checklists in conveyancing on LinkedIn, when making these changes?

Lisa Damon, executive committee member of Seyfarth Shaw, advised – based on her experience – that the most important skill is listening and finding ways to meet fee earners and teams at the stage in the transformation they are in and finding affinity with them.

Help people understand how the new process benefits them personally and the firm in general. A profitable, financially sustainable firm benefits all employees. Follow up with them and check that it is working in the way that everyone anticipated. If it works well, roll out the changes across the firm (if appropriate). If it isn't working well, run through the DMAIC process again to understand what is going wrong and why. Create a story about the change everyone has experienced and the improvements in client experience, profitability or compliance/quality, and share the success story widely.

If those affected by the changes have been involved in the project from the outset and can see the benefits it brings, they are more likely to be supportive. Champions can also be useful to influence teams and departments, as can gamification.

Stage 4 – improvement

Lastly, it is good practice to keep processes under review afterwards in a continuous cycle of questioning and improving.

Ensure that someone is responsible for the process and that they diarise to check it and improve it. Even where a service is well designed, it must be kept under review because the world changes continuously. Technologies are changing at a considerable rate at present. Clients' business needs, their own technologies and experiences are changing, so law firms must continuously adapt their services to suit their needs and the changing competitive landscape.

Improvement cycles

The mapping and streamlining of a small process, particularly for the first time, may involve either breakthrough or continuous improvements.

Breakthrough improvements are radical and tend to come with, say, a new efficient machine in a factory setting or the total redesign of a computer-based system in a service setting; they usually offer sudden step-change improvements.

A law firm could experience such a step-change by replacing disjointed legacy IT systems to create integrated streamlined systems, so that a single input of new starter information feeds into HR systems, financial, internal expert databases, customer relationship management systems, etc., for example.

Continuous improvements tend to improve processes through lots of small, incremental changes. This could be simplifying a sequence or process in a service setting or reducing changeover time on a machine in a factory. Although continuous improvements don't offer a step-change in efficiency, they are often far easier to implement and build on each other.

There are several approaches to continuous improvement (e.g. TQM, Kaizen, Lean, and Six Sigma). There is a summary of these approaches at Appendix 3 and further reading at Appendix 1.

Kaizen is one of the most accessible approaches. This encourages all employees to be responsible for finding small incremental improvements to the way that they work. Everyone should question the status quo: why are they being expected to deliver the service to their client in that manner? What is gained by doing X in that way? Seek the wisdom of the many, rather than rely on the thoughts of the few.

Conclusion

Whilst historically strategic knowledge management and process improvement may not have received the same investment as business development and marketing initiatives, the gap between those law firms which understand the value of knowledge management and process management and those that don't is widening. With significant technological changes due to advances in cognitive computing, artificial intelligence and blockchain in the offing, law firm leaders can no longer afford to ignore the benefits of implementing strategic knowledge management practices, including the process improvement methodologies that other sectors have used so effectively to improve efficiency and profitability. Cultures do not change overnight, so law firms must learn to use these methodologies now in order to become more agile and able to survive the coming sea-change in delivery of legal services.

Appendix 1 – Further reading

Textbooks

Dale, B. (2003) *Managing Quality*, Blackwell: Oxford
George, M. et al (2003) *What is Lean Six Sigma?* McGraw Hill
Russell, H. (2015) *Practical Projects in Legal KM* Worldwide Legal Research
Slack, N. et al (2010) *Operations Management*, Pearson Education: Harlow

Papers, reports and websites

Barnes, H. *Kaizen and the Process of Continuous Improvement in Your Legal Career*, Law Crossing, http://www.lawcrossing.com/article/19/Kaizen-and-the-Process-of-Continuous-Improvement-in-Your-Legal-Career/ (accessed October 2015)
Briefing Magazine, *On Process Management*, October 2012
Hammer, M. (1990) Reengineering Work: Don't automate, Obliterate, *Harvard Business Review*, July-August
ILTA (2014) *Process Innovation*, http://km.iltanet.org/2014/06/02/process-innovation-in-legal-what-it-is-and-how-its-done/ (accessed October 2015)
Legal Services Board (2018) *The legal needs of small businesses* 2013-2017 https://research.legalservicesboard.org.uk/news/latest-research-18/
Seyfarth Shaw (2013) *Applying Lean Six Sigma Methods to Litigation Practice*, http://www.seyfarth.com/dir_docs/publications/LITDecJan2014LeanSixSigma.pdf (accessed October 2015)
www.bpmi.org – website for Business Process Management Initiative
www.quality-foundation.co.uk The British Quality Foundation, a not-for-profit organization promoting business excellence

Appendix 2 – Process map of making a cup of tea

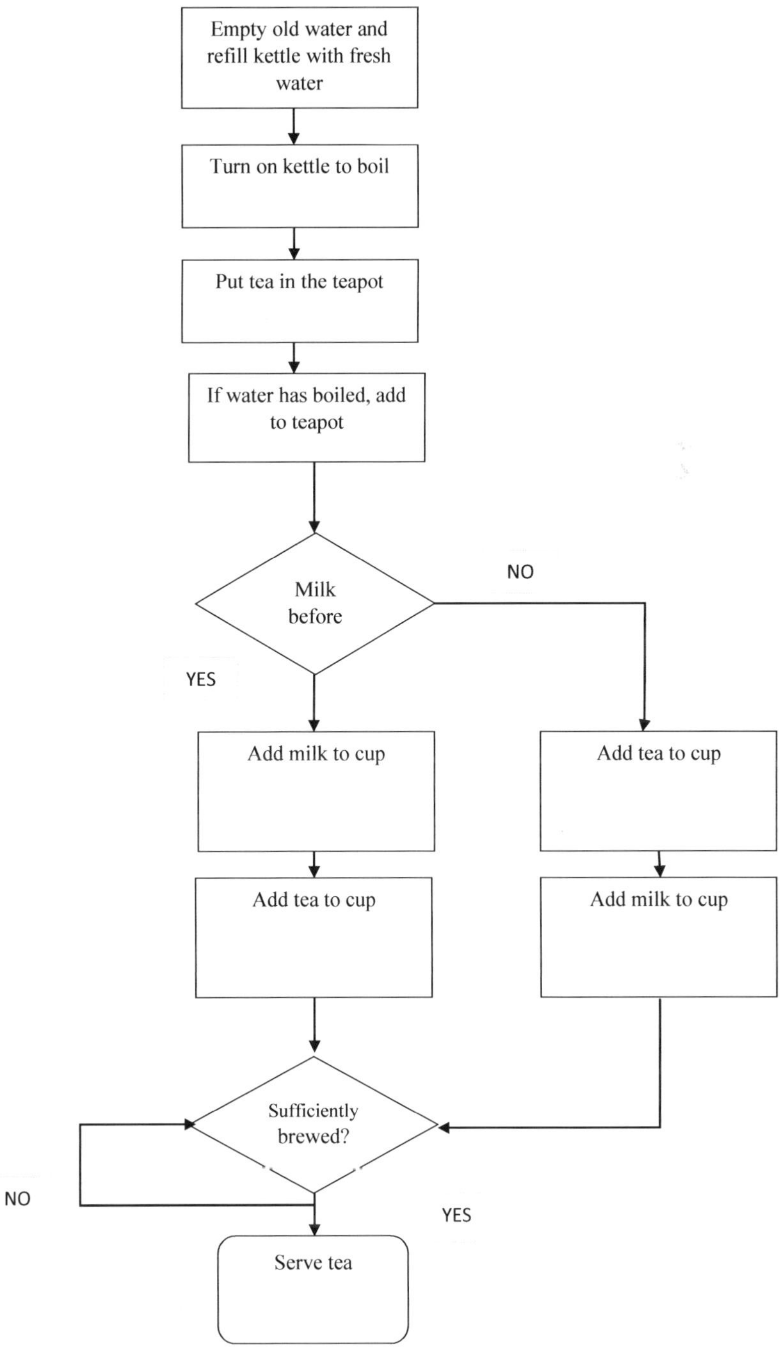

Appendix 3 – Process improvement methodologies

TQM	Places emphasis on: • Meeting and exceeding the needs of clients; • Improving all parts of the organization; • Everyone is included in improvement and success is celebrated; • The costs of quality are all included; • Designing in quality and getting things right first time; and • Developing systems which support improvement.
Lean	Also known as "just-in-time". Initially applied manufacturing, but recently adapted for services too. Aims to meet the demand of clients instantaneously without any waste and with perfect quality - the "goldilocks approach" - neither too much nor too little of anything. Key elements: • Customer-centricity including internal customer-supplier relationships; • Aiming for perfection. synchronizing flow and reducing variations; • Includes everyone; • Eliminating waste.
Six Sigma	A drive towards a virtually zero-defect objective, with a broad improvement concept ("defects" can be in all parts of the process). The levels of expertise are denoted using martial arts terminology, with the most knowledgeable experts known as "Black Belts". Main elements: • The DMAIC improvement cycle - Define, Measure, Analyze, Improve, Control; • Customer-driven objectives; Process design and control; • Use of data/evidence to support changes; • Use of specially trained practitioners.
Kaizen	In Japanese "Kaizen" means improvement all elements of life: personal, work, home and social. When applied to the workplace, it means all workers are involved in process improvements. It doesn't matter if improvements are small, it is the accumulative effect of all the improvements which gain an organization its competitive edge.

Appendix 4 – Fishbone/Ishikawa diagram

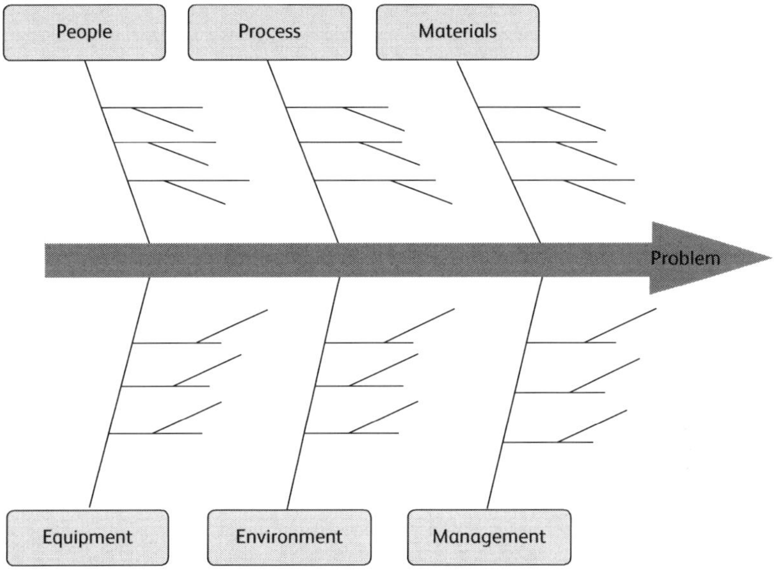

References

1. "The legal needs of small businesses" 2013-2017 (https://research.legalservicesboard.org.uk/news/latest-research-18/).
2. A process map of making a cup of tea is at Appendix 2.
3. David Rueff of Baker Donelson "Becoming a believer" Lexpo 2018, commenting on payment of bills following introduction of BakerLean and BakerManage.
4. Such as "5 Whys" or "Fishbone/Ishikawa diagrams", see Appendix 4.
5. See Appendix 2.
6. Kim Craig formerly of Sayfarth Shaw LLP, "Becoming a believer" Lexpo 2018.

Chapter 4:
Fully loaded or not?

By Peter Lane Secor, director of strategic pricing and project management at Pepper Hamilton LLP

There are numerous ways to calculate profit for clients, matters, timekeepers, practice groups, billing attorneys and more. Regardless of your method, consistency and providing the lowest common denominator, PPPH (profit per partner hour) is vital, fully loaded or not. The key is how you get there. No matter how you do allocations of overhead, the methods will be questioned. A sophisticated approach actually works best. It helps with adoption and acceptance, as when someone questions one number or method, the analyst can point to other metrics which support the same result.

Statement structures

Regardless of method, there are core parts to the profit statement. It starts with revenue: fees received, projected fees or, in some cases, standard value of fees worked. From revenue, however defined, we subtract direct costs, which are attributed to production of revenue: salaries, benefits and write-downs. Revenue minus direct cost is the direct margin or gross margin. Direct margin is a key number because it is considered the "controllable" margin, the direct result of how well engagements are priced and managed. Direct margin shows the impact of discontinuing, utilization and leverage, the associate vs partner ratio. From direct margin we subtract overhead, indirect cost (rent, staff, IT, marketing, management), which results in net margin. Using a fully loaded model, anything above $0 is an addition to PPP (profits per partner); anything below $0 detracts from PPP. Using a cost-only method not including partner compensation, profit distributions – the net margin will be more variable, but has the advantage of being the actual amount partners will put in their pocket and provides a means by which to measure partner profit performance.

	Profit or Contribution Statement	Direct Margin Statement
Revenue	X	X
Direct Costs	X	X
Direct Margin	X	X
DM%	X	X
Overhead	X	
Net Margin	X	
NM%	X	

Figure 1: Statement elements

Cash vs accrual

Beware of cash basis, however – although it is what partners take home, it is a lagging measure. A practice group can look great on a cash basis and can be compensated as such; however, when you switch to an accrual method, the numbers can tell a different story. It is more than likely the start of the next year on a cash basis will be what was reflected by the prior year's accrual model. The primary factors can be changes in utilization or something as simple as the timing of collections.

Standard cost vs actual costs

As referenced, having multiple approaches can take away attorney's abilities to deny profit results. One approach is to present information and amounts using both standard costing and actual costing. For standard costing, cost rates, direct and indirect, should be based on target hours – 1,800 for associates and maybe 1,600 for partners, for example. Actual costing is based on the actual hours worked. With actual costing, the more hours a person works the lower the cost is per hour, even though they are fixed costs which are variable per unit. We are not talking about the old clichés of more hours equals more revenue – as I once heard one partner tell another partner, "being busy means you have to be more efficient". Standard costing is a great way to understand client/matter profitability because it doesn't factor in utilization, aka how busy people are. It instead answers the question of whether work is priced properly, regardless of how busy or not a firm's fee-earners are. The difference between standard costing and actual costing is the utilization adjustment, which provides the dollar value of the impact of utilization. This is a powerful tool for understanding profit for practice groups, industry groups, offices, and more.

The cost-only method

Cost-only methodology comes in a number of varieties:

- No partner compensation and inclusion of overhead;
- The inclusion of full partner compensation and the disregard of overhead; and
- The inclusion of part of partner "earnings," a portion of compensation with or without overhead.

When overhead is not included, the profit statement stops at direct margin, often referenced as a statement of DM (direct margin). If partner compensation is "all in", the DM will then fluctuate widely based on partner compensation – highly compensated partners, senior leadership and rainmakers will consequently never be "profitable". To counter this, the best option is to derive an earnings amount for each partner– perhaps just a certain percentage of compensation, 68 percent for example. A simple method is to just assign one "earnings" amount for all partners regardless of distributions. Back in the spreadsheet-only days, this was very popular; we would look at what partners took home and simply choose an amount to use as compensation for all partners. A more accurate approach is to price by comp band. Most partnerships naturally develop bands of compensation or levels; typically, the size of the partnership determines the number of bands. Similar to the "just pick a number" method, each band is set at a certain earnings amount that is lower than their profit distribution. One other method for two-tiered partnerships, equity and non-equity, is to just assign an amount for each tier. The major advantage of choosing one of these methods is that everyone is measured the same way, thereby making comparable analysis very straightforward. The downside of this is that partners at the bottom compensation levels will feel that the system is unfair. Another cost-only method is to not include any partner comp but to include overhead, aka indirect costs. The margin amount then becomes what partners take home.

The primary value of these cost-only methods is that the results – direct margin or net margin – are "feel good" numbers. Pretty much no one will look unprofitable. There will most likely be a higher level of acceptance, but it will be difficult to fully comprehend the impact of including all compensation, which makes it hard to understand the actual contribution or detraction from profit. This is not as helpful for executive management when having to divide the pie, profits.

Fully loaded method

This is in contrast to a fully loaded profit methodology, which includes all expenses and partner compensation. The largest benefit is the ease of comparability. If the net margin is positive, the group, timekeeper, billing partner, client or matter are all adding to the PPP; if the net margin is negative, the unit is detracting from PPP. Unfortunately, this presents its own set of challenges, which are most often manifested as concerns about the "fairness" of such a system, especially as related to allocation of overhead. Some firms have extremely sophisticated systems for allocating specific expenses. A good is example the cost of marketing. In recent years. firms are dedicating more resources to their marketing efforts. However, percentage-wise, marketing is still a fairly small percentage of the cost of operations – around five percent – and a relatively small piece of the pie. However, in that amount there can be some big individual spends, either by specific partners or as part of other firm initiatives. When someone says, "Why should I be allocated the same as partner X? I didn't use as much marketing as them", it will be necessary to explain the minimal impact and look to the real reasons they have profit issues. The big expense items for firms are often staff and rent. These can be allocated by office, by department, by practice area, and more. Some of the most complicated systems allocate down to the level of looking at office size, square footage, and secretarial ratios – or, indeed, marketing expense – actually used by each partner.

Many methods allocate overhead using weighted full-time equivalencies (FTEs), a weighted FTE allocation. FTEs are the scheduled amount of work, with one being a full-time person and 0.5 being someone who works only half-time. FTEs can also be used over any timeframe. If FTE tracking is done on a monthly basis and a full-time person starts mid-month, their FTE is then 0.5; if a half-time person starts mid-month, their FTE would be 0.25. The same applies if we track FTEs annually.

Month	TK#1	TK#2	TK#3
Jan	-	1.0	1.0
Feb	-	1.0	1.0
Mar	-	1.0	1.0
Apr	1.0	1.0	1.0
May	1.0	1.0	1.0
Jun	1.0	1.0	1.0
Jul	1.0	-	1.0
Aug	1.0	-	1.0
Sep	1.0	-	1.0
Oct	1.0	-	1.0
Nov	1.0	-	1.0
Dec	1.0	-	1.0
TOTAL	9.0	6.00	12.00
Divide by 12 for annual	0.75	0.50	1.00

Figure 2: Annual FTE tracking

We can add weighting to figure out the amount of overhead to allocate to various timekeeper titles. We do this because a first-year associate does not use as much firm resources as a partner. The weighting should not be unbearable – weigh a partner at 4 for a 4 to 1 ratio, for example. The same holds true with setting standard hours. Standard hours should be realistic; these are the standard and not the target hours. As an example, let's say we weigh a partner at 2, an associate at 1, and a paralegal at 0.5. Multiply the FTEs by the weight and divide that into overhead.

Title	FTEs	Weight	Value
Partners	10.0	2.0	20.0
Associates	20.0	1.0	20.0
Paralegals	5.0	0.5	2.5
		Divisor:	42.5

Figure 3: An FTE weighting example

The result is an overhead factor which can be re-weighted against the FTEs. Using the weighted overhead factor method, you can calculate hourly cost rates using standard hours or actual hours. It is a complicated method and can be difficult to explain. This might even be a possible reason not to use a fully loaded margin.

Conclusion

The cost-only methodology is much less complex, especially as you don't have to worry about allocating overhead, let alone "argue" about the results. There is also the "feel good" element; no one looks "bad".

It is a less complicated direct margin schedule – revenues minus direct costs equals direct margin. Good stuff. However, when using cost-only, the comparatives are tougher; what is a good direct margin and what is a bad direct margin number can vary across the different units – clients, matters, practice groups, office, partner and more. You can look to the firm average, compare year over year, or measure against a goal (the firm budget).

Using fully loaded methodology, it is harder to get buy in and is more difficult to calculate, especially if you further complicate it by showing both standard and actual margins. The power of a fully loaded margin is that no one can argue with $0, even you use plus or minus five percent as a guide in the ball park of breakeven after including partner compensation. The model forces the hard decisions – can we keep this client at this level of discounting? Do we need to change the make-up of the group, or change partner compensation levels?

Whichever model you choose, remember that client/matter profitability is a tool to help improve profitability, not a stick, and that behind every profit statement there is a story.

Chapter 5:
Developing and defending a profitability model

By Paige D. Keith, chief financial officer at Hawkins Parnell Thackston & Young, LLP

Imagine the following scenario:

The call came in on a Thursday afternoon at about 2:30 pm from a partner. "We are going to look at profitability," he said. "We need to present it to the partnership at the next quarterly meeting. Thanks." Three months later, he sat at a conference room table staring at some numbers on a screen.

"Those numbers can't possibly be right," he exclaimed in disbelief. "You didn't include this, did you? The software you chose can't calculate this the way we need it to, correct? You didn't even consider allocating expenses in a way that would be fairer, right? And you can't say within reasonable certainty that this is even accurate, can you," he asked, not pausing for answers. Shaking his head, he muttered to himself, "There is no way I can show these numbers to my partners."

In the past decade, many law firms have recognized that examining profitability beyond the income statements is essential to the growth and longevity of the firm. Hundreds of blog posts, articles, white papers and books address the need, methods, pitfalls and benefits of profitability tools and models. Even with these resources, partnerships often jump into profitability without clear purpose and understanding, resulting in countless failures and general mistrust of profitability reports. If developed and managed carefully, methods and models implemented under the consensus of the partnership can provide invaluable data, helping the partnership improve the bottom line and establish competitive advantages in the legal marketplace. This chapter examines steps to ensure that a firm partnership accepts and implements profitability models and methods to mitigate dissension and potential failures.

Include partners in the development of profitability models

To an accounting or finance professional, profitability is academic and simple:

$$\text{Revenue} - \text{expenses} = \text{profit}$$

To a partner in a law firm, profitability is personal. It is their livelihood and the measure of their professional success. Profits buy their homes and send their kids to school. The likelihood of the partnership completely trusting something so personal to someone who is not one of their own is rare.

Lawyers are lawyers. They have spent their careers trying to be good lawyers. Most lawyers did not go to law school because they want to become finance experts. Consequently, most attorneys do not enjoy discussing profitability models. This lack of interest often leads firms to task their finance professionals with development and implementation of profitability models. At first this makes sense – outsource the task to the experts. However, with a 10 percent margin on a report next to their name – or even worse, a negative sign before a number – previously disengaged partners suddenly have copious amounts of time to point out flaws in the firm's profit methodology. When profitability is viewed as an indictment on their practice, some partners refuse to acknowledge the objective truth in simple numbers.

To remedy this skepticism, firms must get partner buy-in on the front end by including key partners on a profitability committee. The choice of profitability committee members invariably decides the outcome of a debate about profitability model acceptance. Some firms might choose just one or two partners with established reputations to sit on the committee. Others might choose partners from each of its offices or practice groups. Objective qualifications, such as high revenue or financial training, should not automatically qualify a partner to serve on a profitability committee. Ideally, the firm should select partners invested in the firm's future who are willing to learn the intricacies that color profitability and who can effectively advocate the use of profitability in business decisions. The firm should task the partners along with finance professionals with:

1. Vetting and choosing a profitability software

The purpose of this chapter is not to sponsor any specific software. Firms have unique desires from profitability tools and software. Sometimes a spreadsheet provides a simple yet firm foundation for calculating profitability, but higher volumes of data and complexities often create need for more robust tools. The partnership should consider these tools an investment.

Finance professionals are often best suited to select the proper software based on guidance from firm management. However, without key partner inclusion in this decision, some partners will invariably believe that it is the software, not the objective data, that makes their practice appear unprofitable.

Having partners as part of the software selection team diminishes the importance of the particular computer program chosen. Software is simply a calculator, not a decision maker.

2. Choosing the methods for allocating revenue and expenses

Allocating expenses and revenue is like choosing a house to buy. There are several options on the market, but everyone has needs, wants, and desires. Like many things in life, compromise is the precursor to progress.

A finance professional values practicality and profitability. A partner seeks an affirmation that their work is profitable. A finance professional may examine the transactional costs of allocation at a certain level in the terms of money and time to determine the level at which an expense allocated. Attorneys partner may argue for allocation of expenses on a very detailed level, attempting allocate expenses in the most precise manner possible.

Compromise between extreme detail in expense measurement and practicability of calculation is critical before presenting a model to the partnership. Practicality reduces time and increases efficiencies at the cost of total accuracy. Conversely, allocating expenses on the most cellular level increases accuracy but sacrifices efficiency.

Having partners who are willing to understand this tradeoff helps create a model that provides enough accurate data to base decisions but eliminates the time consumption of counting the proverbial "ceiling tiles".

3. Implementing policies and processes that alleviate ambiguity

Profitability is a dense subject. There are depths of revenue and expenses that can be rabbit holes. The purpose of assigning partners to a profitability committee is to keep other partners from diving down these holes in search of answers to immaterial questions

One key to eliminating this behavior is to implement policies regarding defining data. Firms can define critical data in a number of ways, and accounting software implements these important decisions. For example, firms can define timekeepers as working attorney, billing attorney, matter billing attorney, matter responsible attorney, originating attorney, etc. Policies that set precedent for defining these roles create consistency in data. Further, policies that require defining data from timekeeper roles, matter types, practice group, payors, insurance carriers, etc., create accountability at client intake that carries through to profitability. A partner who has a relationship with clients can understand the need for and ensures compliance with the firm's policies. This yields not only better profitability data and forecasts, but also data points for matter management.

4. Becoming advocates for the methods and uses of profitability metrics

Naysayers of profitability determinations are less likely to "shoot the messenger" of a profitability analysis if there is firm buy-in on the methodology, which can be achieved with an effective profitability committee. Although finance professions provide critical analysis capable of securing a firm's financial future, our analysis is only as effective as its acceptance. Partners listen to their partners. They are the engine for profitability buy-in, which gives meaning and life to the analysis performed by finance professionals. At the risk of sounding repetitive, profitability is personal to partners. Like many aspects of our lives, it is hard to question the analysis when it comes from someone we trust. If a respected partner trusts the profitability methodology, other partners are more likely to appreciate the value of profitability data rather than question its validity.

Use a case study for the initial roll out

Generally, partners dislike being told their book of business is unprofitable or that their book of business should be more. Using the profitability model to identify profitable and unprofitable partners upon implementation will most likely create reluctance and animosity towards it. However, if partners accepted and validated the model for another purpose on a previous occasion, they will have less arguments against it when used for more sensitive purposes. Some single case studies that may generate better reception may include: using profitability for specific matter management; evaluating a pricing structure such as an alternative fee arrangement on a specific client; making staffing decisions on a new client or evaluating margins; and staffing on a single partner's book of business. Benefits of case studies include the ability:

1. To validate a model on a small scale before large scale implementation

Profitability methods and models have many components making up revenue and expenses with multiple scenarios available to run on each, making the simple equation "revenue – expenses = profit" quite complex. Inevitably, one may miss small nuances that impact profitability in an initial roll out. A small case study exposes these nuances so that one can adjust the models to accommodate them.

2. To test methods of reporting profitability

Spreadsheets are valuable tools for the purpose of calculating profitability and profitability margins. However, spreadsheets are not the best tool in producing results of profitability analysis. For a profitability model and method to be purposeful, it needs to be translated from a chart of numbers to a story with an ending still to write. Small scale implementations permit the firm to determine how to tell that story and who should tell it.

3. To create a success story to achieve further buy-in

A successful roll out on each small-scale case study begets another successful roll out. Ultimately, success in these multiple case studies validate the model and methodology, allowing it to be further implemented on the more sensitive issues such as identifying profitable and unprofitable partners and compensation.

Indoctrinate partnership regularly and consistently

The famous basketball coach John Wooden once said,

> *"The four laws of learning are explanation, demonstration, imitation and repetition. The goal is to create a correct habit that can be produced instinctively under great pressure. To make sure this goal was achieved, I create eight laws of learning — namely explanation, demonstration, imitation, repetition, repetition, repetition, repetition, and repetition."*

The firm needs and wants the partnership to create the habit of valuing profitability and using it to make better business decisions. Some partners will use a lack of understanding of the theory behind a model to discredit its value, while others may overly complicate the math to distract from the results. It is incumbent on the profitability committee to ensure partners understand and accept profitability models. Profitability analysis will never generate the excitement and interest of March Madness, but with John Wooden's approach, profitability should capture the attention of any partnership.

1. Explanation

Partners converted to an appreciation of profitability can become effective advocates. Partners involved in the development of the profitability model become the teachers. They develop resource materials including references, white papers and presentations to use as the textbooks to understanding profitability. The lawyers on the committee can help the finance team translate the conceptual language of finance to the practical vernacular of a legal practice.

2. Demonstration

Law firm profitability is not a new frontier needing exploration and settlement. Many law firms have relied on profitability metrics for decades. Records of successes and failures and evaluating law firm profitability exist in multitude. Firms should use these stories – available through books, conference materials, articles, blog posts, etc. – to demonstrate the necessity and power of profitability models. Dialogue between firms grappling with similar issues can be the vehicle of progress, as many face the same obstacles.

3. Imitation

Realizing other firms successfully implement profitability models and use them to make business decisions will inspire the firm to imitate those best practices in developing their own model and usage. Understanding that an industry has already developed general theory and processes adds validity to the firm's current model. Adopting these proven best practices can develop strong models that are understandable, modifiable and purposeful, ultimately leading to a firm's own success.

4. Repetition, repetition, repetition, repetition

Law firms should regularly send its partners articles about profitability analysis written by thought leaders. Similarly, law firms should repeat the cycle of explaining and demonstrating profit successes and failures to its partnership regularly. It can do this by holding seminars on a regular basis. Lateral partners must understand the value the firm places of profitability immediately. Most importantly, once the partnership understands and starts using profitability in decisions such as compensation, it should explain and demonstrate the accepted profitability models to its associates who may one day be partners.

Acknowledge limitations of the model

A key component in gaining consensus among the firm partners is acknowledging the limitations of the model. A profitability model is not a "magic eight ball" that quickly and succinctly answers the questions that plague law firms. It is instead more like a flashlight, a tool that shines light on areas where firms can improve their bottom line. Law firms develop models based on a set of assumptions consistent with the culture, industry and best practices at that time. As time moves forward, the assumptions once used to develop the model may no longer be true, and models must change to reflect new assumptions.

As previously mentioned, firms may choose to sacrifice perfection for practicality and efficiency. In cross-examination lawyers try to disprove absolutes. Claiming a model is perfect opens the door to unnecessary cross-examination. Acknowledging these limitations does not render a model insufficient, useless or incorrect. Instead, acknowledging the limitations shows a full understanding of how and when the model can be applied or where other metrics outside of profitability may be needed to create a complete picture.

Conclusion

The ability to limit criticism and gain acceptance of profit models ultimately determines the validity and ability to use the model in business decisions. By including partners in the development of the model, by methodically gaining acceptance and by regularly educating the partnership on profitability and the financial theories behind the model, firms can lessen the criticism levied by mistrustful partners.

Chapter 6:
In favor of a client- and product-focused profitability analysis

By Thomas W. Van Der Moere, chief financial officer at Neal, Gerber & Eisenberg LLP

Companies consistently face challenges and opportunities to enhance their business models and provide value to their customers, workforce and owners. Law firms, of course, are no different. Firms need to address competition (for clients and talent) from traditional and non-traditional providers of legal services. They must grapple with the economic forces of supply and demand for legal products and services, as well as the complexity of responding to those forces through pricing and acquiring and maintaining the optimum mix and depth of talent. Firms face pressures to reshape their compensation structures to provide incentives that motivate a level of profitability that attracts, rewards and retains key business generators and the workforce required to effectively support that business. In order to remain viable and competitive, a firm must decide where and how best to invest its limited available resources (i.e., its retained earnings/capital/debt) in technology, marketing, infrastructure, geographic presence, and talent. A firm that has a well-defined, flexible, and clearly understood profitability methodology, a culture that embraces a profitability mindset, and the ability to fully leverage that methodology when making decisions will be better prepared to take advantage of strategic challenges and opportunities it faces.

This chapter will focus on a law firm's opportunity to analyze existing and potential business using client and product profitability analysis. Too often, firms develop and deploy systems that are tilted toward a focus on analyzing the productivity of (billable hour) and revenue contributed by timekeepers (individually or in the aggregate). Realigning that focus on the profitability of clients and the products the firm offers to its clients will lead to strategic insights into the factors/characteristics that are correlated with more profitable aspects of the firm's business. Understanding which revenue dollars drive firm profits and why will allow the firm to concentrate its efforts and direct its resources where the return on those resources can be maximized.

Client and product profitability – developing a methodology

As law firms build their understanding and sophistication in leveraging profitability analysis, its impact should be felt in several areas. Profitability analysis should affect talent acquisition and retention decisions. It should also influence the retention of clients and the acceptance of new clients. Compensation systems should be informed by contribution to the firm's profitability. The pricing of engagements and the overall pricing strategy of the firm require a deep understanding of the impact on profitability. Even the delivery of legal services to clients has to consider such factors of profitability as the efficiency and staffing mix of the service delivered, in addition to the quality of service delivered and the responsiveness of the law firm to its clients' needs.

A well-designed methodology that is deployed for a variety of purposes throughout the firm will also provide the added benefit of identifying opportunities to improve practices or address behavior issues that directly impact firm profitability.

Understanding how profitability will impact performance measurement and decision-making throughout the firm will guide the development and refinement of the firm's profitability methodology. The illustration below presents a typical profitability methodology that can be used at the firm, practice group, product, client or even individual timekeeper level. This conceptual diagram is also a way to illustrate – not only to attorneys, but also to administrative department leadership and finance staff – how each member of staff can directly or indirectly impact the profitability of the firm.

This methodology begins with some concept of the fee-generating capacity applicable to what is being measured. This can be defined a number of ways, depending on the operations of the firm, but the conceptually simple calculation is to determine the hours capacity available multiplied by the average standard billing rate offered to clients (full-time equivalent timekeepers x the standard billable hours expectations for the timekeepers x the timekeepers' standard billing rate).

All firms experience a leakage of that fee capacity from a variety of sources. Timekeepers that are undisciplined recorders of time fail to capture all of the effort they spend on a client's matter or even self-discount their time (from the unease at appearing as inefficient) by not recording time for which they perceive the client will not pay or will challenge.

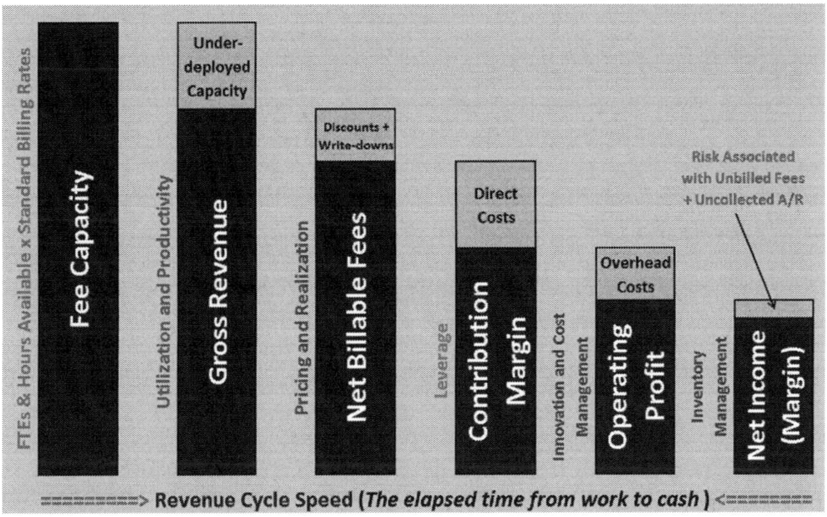

Figure 1: General segments of a profitability methodology

Leakage of fee capacity can also be derived from how resources are managed and deployed throughout the firm. Larger practice areas within a firm may suffer from being a loosely-connected group of solo practitioners, even if those practitioners are essentially delivering the same product to clients. If each practitioner requires their own team to service clients, and there is no disciplined resource management practice in place to ensure that available resources are fully utilized across the practice, it is likely that almost all timekeepers are contributing some level of fee capacity leakage that, when added up across the practice, is significant lost profit potential. Don't get me wrong – 100 percent or greater utilization of a firm's resources is highly unlikely and probably not desirable over the long run. Having an appropriate level of bench strength in certain practices is also required in situations where client demand can be volatile or is needed to maintain a perceived ability to handle larger client matters. However, a more disciplined approach to managing the allocation of work among available resources to ensure they are sufficiently utilized will have a material impact on the firm's profit.

The next factor in the profitability continuum are the fee discounts agreed to with clients and the writing-down of fees prior to preparing the invoice to the client. The result is the net billable fees that the firm passes on to clients.

As noted at the bottom of the chart shown above, profitability is impacted by the work-to-cash cycle time. Often referred to as bill-speed and collection-speed, this is the amount of time that elapses from when the work was performed to when the firm receives payment for their services from clients. The speed at which recorded time is converted to billed fees and the billed fees are converted to cash received by the firm can have direct profitability implications as well as indirect consequences. Because of the need to carry this investment related to unconverted work-to-cash, if a firm needs to draw upon its line of credit to fund continuing operations the borrowing costs will be a direct overhead expense. The speed of this conversion could also create a requirement for partner capital investment or could result in delayed distributions of profit to the partners.

Costs come from direct sources associated with the firm's revenue producers (partner salaries, non-partner attorney and paralegal compensation, benefits and payroll taxes paid by the firm) and indirect sources or overhead (i.e., the costs to operate the firm such as occupancy costs, administrative department costs, professional liability insurance, etc.). A good profitability model can assist in highlighting where leverage, staffing mix, and compensation adjustments could improve profit margins by better aligning costs with the firm's revenue potential. A profitability model can not only inform revenue producers of the firm as to where opportunities exist to improve client and product profitability, but it can also be used by administrative department management to better understand how the processes and costs that they manage have a significant impact on the firm's profitability. Tying the impact of process improvement initiatives, innovation, technology enhancements, and cost management programs back to the profitability of client engagements, practices and the firm is powerful support for the projects, initiatives and resources requested by the firm's administrative support departments.

Lastly, leakage of potential revenue comes from: 1) the write-off of uncollected accounts receivable and 2) time and costs that age as work-in-process and are eventually written off. Good inventory management practices that include frequent monitoring, measurement and notification of potential issues, as well as a collaborative and coordinated effort between your firm's finance staff and billing attorneys, is essential to limiting the impact of this material profit leak.

The table below provides a simple illustration of the basic methodology that could apply to results at the firm, practice, office, client/matter, product or timekeeper level.

Timekeeper FTEs	300		85 Equity Partners
Hours Available	525,000		
Fee Capacity (@ Std Rates)	$263,000,000	$500	Weighted average of all timekeepers' standard rates
Unused Capacity	80,000	15%	
	($40,000,000)		
Gross Revenue (@ Std Rates)	$223,000,000	445,000	Client billable hours
Discounts & Write-downs	($33,000,000)	(15%)	
Net Billable Fees	$190,000,000		
Direct Costs	($90,000,000)	(40%)	*Assumes average base direct cost per Equity Partner of $350,000*
Contribution Margin	$100,000,000		
Overhead Costs	($70,000,000)	(31%)	
Operating Profit	$30,000,000		
Client Investment Costs	($4,500,000)	(2%)	*Time that remains unbilled, uncollected A/R, cost/disbursement write-offs, etc.*
Net Income (Margin)	$25,500,000	11%	

Figure 2: A basic profitability calculation

Client and product profitability analysis

In most law firms today, you will hear varying levels of discussion about and claims that they are client-focused and provide their clients with quality service. This should be a priority for law firms. Competition for client business is fierce. Non-traditional service providers are entering the market, as they see opportunities to take market share from traditional law firms and do so profitably. Clients are much more sophisticated and aggressive in their procurement of legal services and demand more value from their providers. Clients want different prices for different products provided by their law firms based on the value they receive from those products.

Despite this shift in focus to the client and the products they consume, many law firm financial and practice management systems are rooted primarily in the firm, practice groups and departments, offices and regions, and attorneys/timekeepers rather than clients and the firm's products. Some of this is driven by traditional accounting-based roll-ups of cost and revenue centers as well as partner compensation and other incentive systems. Any client-focused analysis tends to stop at revenue and revenue in process (accounts receivable and unbilled time). Product analysis, if done, is likely to only have a revenue-based focus, and is most likely in response to developing an alternative fee arrangement requested by a client.

The constant struggle to grow demand and revenue, in part to absorb the timekeeper capacity that many firms have maintained as well as the pricing pressures exerted by clients, has clouded the focus on profitability somewhat. Intuitively, law firm leaders realize that not all dollars of revenue contribute an equal amount of profit to the firm. However, firms' profitability models and analyses need to shift the focus to understanding that statement in the context of their clients and the firm's products. A system that facilitates this analysis across the firm's existing client base, its various types of matters/services from its practices, and acceptance of new client business will position the firm to better address the profit leakages discussed above, better inform pricing and fee arrangements, create clearer understanding of the underlying cost drivers in the delivery of legal services, and inform decisions as to which and what types of clients and mix of firm services require the firm's resources and continued investment.

These client- and product-focused profitability models must highlight:

- Differences in the prices charged to different clients;
- Discounts or other forms of revenue support required by clients;
- Differences in the products/services delivered to different clients;
- Differences in the amount of resources consumed across clients;
- Whether the firm is working with decision-makers at the client or if decisions need to be made up the chain of command;
- The level of support required by clients (do some require large teams? Are some clients less sophisticated or require more touch points? What is the breadth and focus of the client's internal legal team?); and
- The industries in which firm clients operate (are there common characteristics/factors that drive client or product profitability by industry?).

The direct benefits of client- and product-profitability analysis lie in the insight it provides in the uneven distribution of revenue and costs among clients and the firm's products. The insight gained from this analysis regarding the extent to which specific customers, types of customers, and products consume the firm's resources should generate opportunities for the firm in better management of costs, better informed pricing and revenue generation, and concentrated strategic marketing activities.

Considerations for developing a profitability methodology for clients and products

I do not plan to address basic design elements of a profitability model and system, as that is addressed substantially in a number of texts and articles (for example, the best method to use to allocate overhead costs). However, there are several key elements that deserve mention as they will help develop a model that facilitates client and product profitability analysis. Overall, you need to design a model and system that is flexible, and can be customized and adjusted to fit how you want to use it within your firm. Make sure you have thought through your data sources (general ledger, payroll system, other external sources of cost, revenues, full-time equivalents, etc.) and have developed a mapping to your profitability system that contains the level of granularity (or summarization) that fits your particular firm's needs. For example, if your model includes an extensive breakdown of overhead costs, you may invite greater debate from your attorneys on whether they are a consumer of that cost to the same extent as another attorney.

Some of the areas that have particular relevance to client and product profitability analysis are the measurement period basis, how you factor in partner compensation, the need for reconciling the profit data to your general ledger, product designations and cost rates.

Measurement period basis

An important distinction to make in the profitability model for analyzing client and product profitability is the basis to use for the measurement period. The accounting rule of matching revenues with costs applies here as well. The two basic periods to consider are the "worked period" and the "collected period". The worked period basis focuses on the costs that are associated with the work done (recorded) during the measurement period. The collected period basis focuses on the revenue (fees collected) during the measurement period.

Since the worked period basis starts with the actual time recorded and costs incurred, you must identify the revenues directly associated with that time/cost. Depending on when you are analyzing the worked period data, the associated revenues are likely in different stages of being converted to cash:

- A portion of the time/fees has been billed and collected (revenue);
- A portion of the time/fees has been billed, but remains uncollected (accounts receivable); and
- A portion of the time/fees remains unbilled (work-in-process).

Given the last two stages represent a transition to cash, you must develop assumptions that reflect some degree of risk that the amounts do not convert to cash/revenue. Although you could choose to develop your model to exclude inventory (A/R and WIP) from revenue, it probably does not make sense to do so for client and product profitability analysis (it may, if you feel it is appropriate for individual timekeeper or practice group profitability – creating an incentive to collect). For client and product profitability, determining some methodology for setting collection risk and billing risk to apply to time/fees that are in the A/R and WIP stages, respectively, is most effective. A basic methodology involves an analysis of historical realizations and/or the likely conversion to cash based on the historical aging of the firm's/client's A/R and WIP.

The collected period basis starts with revenue (fees collected) produced in the measurement period. If you use the costs from the measurement period, you will not achieve a matching of costs and revenue (i.e. different costs were incurred to produce the revenue you are collecting in the measurement period) – not ideal for meaningful client and product profitability analysis. You must, therefore, try to develop a methodology that identifies costs associated to the period from which the revenue originated. When write-downs occurred or A/R and WIP still exist related to that revenue, you must be certain your methodology is not over- or under-allocating costs to the measurement period and misstating profitability.

For the purposes of client and product profitability, the worked period basis would tend to be the preferable method, because of the importance of understanding the true amount of effort and cost absorbed in servicing the client and delivering the product during the measurement period.

Partner compensation

Should partner compensation (draws/distributions/bonuses) be considered a cost or is it just profit? For client and product profitability (and maybe for most law firm profitability models), I think it makes sense to include some portion of what a partner receives as a direct cost to the profitability model. Most firms should be able to agree upon a reasonable amount to associate to a partner as a direct salary cost. This direct salary cost does not have to be, and in most cases should not be, the partners' draw amount. The amount of the partners' total compensation and the direct salary cost can be captured separately and included if important to the type of profitability analysis that is being performed. For client and product profitability, any compensation above the direct salary cost should be excluded. Including the profit that was produced during the measurement period as a cost to the client or product being analyzed distorts the results.

Reconciliation of the profitability model to the general ledger

In the abstract, reconciling your profitability data to the income statement generated from your general ledger sounds like a prudent exercise to ensure the data's accuracy. Your controller will likely roll his or her eyes at the suggestion that you would not do so. However, you should seriously consider not forcing a reconciliation to the general ledger. Of course, it will depend on the types of profitability analyses you will be performing and whether or not your organization requires that the two sets of data tie out perfectly.

Here are some benefits and issues related to each:

	Benefit	Issue
Reconciliation	• Reconciliation to the income statement may help obtain buy-in from skeptical partners about the accuracy of the profitability data you are relating to them, their clients, their practice, etc.	• There may be costs that you do not want to include in profitability analyses. For example, one-time charges or other costs incurred that are not part of normal operations. • There are likely to be frequent situations where you may want to spread the impact of certain costs over multiple periods for profitability analysis. For example, if you wish to include in your profitability model any bonuses paid to associates or staff, which are paid (and hit the GL) in December, you may want to spread these amounts over an entire calendar year period. • Some firms may want to reflect certain revenues as an offset to expenses (i.e., any revenue produced by the billing of library research staff related to a client engagement is offset against the cost of that administrative area).
No Reconciliation	• Flexibility through fewer restrictions on how you use various components of revenue and cost to inform the profitability model and leverage it for multiple purposes.	• Being prepared to easily explain how not tying out exactly to the firm's financial statement net income is OK and is unnecessary to effectively use the results of the profitability models.

Product designations

Law firms have products to sell. Those products are developed through varied processes (using different resources and costs), are often priced differently, are marketed differently, and present widely varying client demand scenarios for firms. Consequently, they contribute to a law firm's revenue and profitability uniquely as well. We should, therefore, measure the profit contribution of those products to better assess which products carry the highest margin potential and where opportunities for cost efficiencies, tailored pricing, and demand creation exist.

It is strongly encouraged that you develop a set of product codes (or areas of practice or however the firm wishes to label them) that you attach as part of the metadata you assign to matter records. These should be matter designations that represent unique categories of matters on which you typically work for your clients. If you make the designation too broad, it will become difficult to wade through the volume of data (i.e., time records) to isolate the drivers of effort/cost for the matter. You may also lose the ability to better identify opportunities to price the stages or phases of a matter differently, which may give you an edge in securing work from a client or in demonstrating value more clearly. For example, if your only product designation for corporate and securities matters was a single "corporate" designation, you are potentially restricting your ability to fully understand the underlying cost drivers of this collection of engagements with clients. By grouping your matters into slightly more specific segments – such as M&A, public company securities, venture capital, etc. – you have an opportunity (perhaps coupled with some well-defined and easy to implement matter phase/task codes) to cost and price work that aligns with what your client sees as your product offering to them. The extension is to then analyze the relative profit contribution of various product segments or of the profit contribution of a single product across the client base. A practice that has the ability to analyze the pattern of effort and cost to deliver its products, will more readily be able to identify opportunities to increase efficiency and reduce costs, and, in turn, have the confidence and flexibility to offer fee arrangements to better meet their clients' value expectations.

Cost rates (standard vs full)

As client and product profitability analysis is reliant on the underlying cost data and assumptions, establishing a basis for cost rates is important to the methodology. Cost rate data not only informs the analysis of historical results, but is important in developing predictive models of profitability and "what-if" planning scenarios. So, should cost rates be based on a pre-defined number of standard hours per timekeeper? In other words, should we create a standard-cost rate that ignores whether one timekeeper is "busier" or more fully deployed than another? Alternatively, should cost rates be based on the actual hours worked by a timekeeper? Some firms refer to this as a full-cost rate because it includes the cost of carrying excess capacity (the difference between a standard hours target and actual hours recorded).

Although the full-cost rate has its purpose, it should not necessarily be used for client and product profitability analysis. The full-cost rate is useful in situations where you are analyzing the profitability of an organizational unit (i.e., the working results of a practice group or the firm as a whole) or an individual working timekeeper.

For most client and product profitability analyses, the standard-cost rate approach provides for stronger comparability across clients and products. In other words, two attorneys with identical salaries and benefits and billing rates would produce the same amount of profit per hour recorded, regardless of whether one was 100 percent utilized and the other was 80 percent utilized. The standard-cost rate approach does not penalize or burden a client or product with the cost associated with carrying excess capacity within a practice or across the firm.

Having spent some time discussing conceptually the uses of client and product profitability analysis as well as considerations in developing a methodology, let's take a look at a simple case study that provides a basis for leveraging client and product profitability analysis to support business decision-making.

Case study

The following case study provides some insight into the mechanics of implementing client and product profitability analysis. The firm in the case study – Van Treist, McCallen & Holland – is a fictitious 300-timekeeper firm principally based in Minneapolis, but with several offices in the Midwest and an office in the Miami area. The firm has transactional- and controversy-based practices and a broad and diversified client base. The clients represent many industries and are a mix of public and privately held companies and individuals.

The last eight weeks had been some of the most unpleasant time of Susan Driver's career. The annual compensation process for the partners of the firm had just wrapped up and final bonus compensation had been disclosed to partners almost a week prior. The discussions during (and outside of) the compensation committee meetings had, in many cases, been particularly contentious and personal. The bonus pool was smaller this past year, and had been gradually declining for the past four to five years. Some areas of the firm were doing fairly well, maintaining or increasing revenue slightly. However, other areas were experiencing slight to moderate pressure on demand for services and lower overall revenues per client. As with many firms their size, the firm was also struggling to manage increasing costs, the need to invest in technology and business development, and manage overcapacity across the firm.

These factors were all contributing to an uneasiness throughout the partner ranks and was clearly behind the difficulties experienced during this year's compensation discussions.

Sitting in her office in the evening of another long day, the firm's managing partner reread a couple of emails she had received earlier in the day from two of the firm's prominent partners. The first email was from Mark Janseits, the co-leader of the litigation practice:

> *"Many of the partners in this practice that I have talked to over the last several days are very displeased with their final compensation for the year, and raised concerns over the lack of growth of our firm in both demand for our services and the income available to the partnership. Although I do not think that any of them are immediate 'flight risks', I think we need to take steps to better understand what we need to do to improve our results as a firm and retain our top talent. Our focus should be on revenue generation. Perhaps it is time to more significantly raise our billing rates, even if it means our realizations will drop a bit further than they have already. I think we also just need to tell people to get off their chairs and go get more business. We also seem a bit heavy on administrative staff – a little more cost-cutting can't hurt. Let me know what I can do to help."*

The second email had come from Laura Dennison. Laura and Susan had joined the same large multi-national law firm as associates over 20 years ago. They both left that firm around the same time. Laura went in-house at a former client, while Susan went to another large law firm, eventually landed at Van Treist, McCallen & Holland (VMH) about 12 years ago and became managing partner in 2016. Laura was recruited by Susan last year to lead the firm's private equity practice. Susan had always respected Laura's opinion and often sought her perspective on various issues she encountered in both her practice and in managing the firm. Laura wrote:

> *"I know you are probably bearing the brunt of the grumbling about the results of this year's partner compensation – I know I'm hearing my fair share! Don't get discouraged. Look, I think under your leadership, we have truly started to turn the focus of the firm towards the keys for improving our competitive position in the marketplace – emphasizing productivity and innovation, bringing structure and focus to our business development efforts, investing in technology and talent to meet our clients' needs, improving client communication, etc. These take time to bear fruit of course... and we at VMH are not the most patient folks in the world.*

And at least the concept of profitability has entered our lexicon and we've started to calculate it in terms of individual partner and practice group performance. However, I think we need to take it to the next level. We need to realize that not every dollar of revenue we collect from our clients contributes equally to the firm's profits. I'll be the first to admit that I have taken on some clients that consume a lot of my and my team's time, but for a small amount of fees or at a steep discount. But when we are measured heavily on the hours and revenue we generate, our perspectives (and decisions) get distorted. What I'm trying to say is that maybe our focus should shift from our practice groups, offices, and individual partners to our clients and the products/services we offer them. Which clients and services contribute (or could potentially contribute) higher profit margins to the firm and why? If we can then leverage that analysis to divert our resources to attracting and retaining like clients or deliver our services more profitably, how can our results not improve? I'd love to hear what your thoughts are on this."

Throughout the day, Susan had been jotting down her thoughts about what the firm should do and came to a similar conclusion – a greater focus on the firm's clients and the firm's products and how they contribute to overall profitability was probably a good place to start. As Mark suggested, rate adjustments, building better business development capabilities throughout the firm, and cost management certainly should to some extent be addressed. However, Susan was persuaded by Laura's idea to look at the profitability of the firm's clients and products. Would it not potentially yield the information necessary to identify opportunities for the firm to improve results, as well as informing more targeted adjustments to pricing, where to focus the firm's business development efforts, and better utilize resources and costs? She formulated those thoughts into four goals for the firm, leveraging profitability analysis:

- An improved understanding of the firm's sources of profitability;
- An improved understanding of the relationship between the characteristics of clients, products and costs;
- An improved understanding of the relationship between behaviors of timekeepers, staff and costs; and
- Better informed decisions about the allocation of resources to clients, types of clients, and products.

As Susan packed up for the evening commute home, she considered her next steps. On the ride home she wondered whether the firm had the systems, capabilities and data to undertake this type of analysis. Later that night she sent a meeting notice to her heads of operations and finance to better understand what it would take to accomplish her objectives.

Response to case study

Susan and VMH are struggling with what most other law firms, to varying degrees, are facing. Simply raising rates is no longer a sustainable long-term strategy to increase profit. Firms have or are addressing fixed and variable overhead costs. Getting their arms around how and what clients and the products they purchase contribute value to the firm is an essential undertaking for any firm looking to compete in today's legal industry. To start this process at VMH, Susan and her team should follow this basic framework for their client and product profitability initiative:

- Selection of existing clients and products;
- Design the profitability model;
- Calculate the client and product profitability;
- Interpret the profitability results; and
- Establish the ability to perform client and product profitability analysis on a consistent, repeatable and regular basis.

Susan's goals for the firm's profitability analysis study are appropriately focused on obtaining the information she and the firm's leaders need to begin to understand which clients and products consume the firm's resources and where those resources have an uneven relationship to the revenues they generate. Identifying the targets for cost management and profit improvement initiatives that will contribute the most significant opportunities to impact the firm's profitability is the direct benefit of a client- and product-driven profitability analysis. Those clients that are highly profitable must be retained. Small, unprofitable customers that have limited potential to improve or grow (i.e., lead to more profitable work) should be referred to firms more suited to service the client. Small or less profitable clients (with potential to grow into more profitable clients) may require development programs to improve their profit contribution to the firm. This analysis can be similarly applied to the firm's products, and can be especially informative if it can be accomplished in combination with the client's that procure them.

Susan should consider forming a team that includes marketing, finance, knowledge management and, if appropriate and manageable, select attorneys. From there, the first step will be a thorough review of the firm's current active clients. A good place to start may be to try to segment clients based on some measure of volume/size and profitability. The table below is an example of a simple segmentation of the VMH firm data based on client size.

	Large	Mid-sized	Small	TOTAL
Number of Clients	100	250	1,500	1,850
Billable Hours Generated	180,000	160,000	90,000	430,000
Fees @ Std Rates	$125,000,000	$100,000,000	$55,000,000	$280,000,000
Fees Generated	$110,000,000	$82,000,000	$44,000,000	$236,000,000
Avg Std Rate	$690	$630	$610	$650
Avg Effective Rate	$610	$510	$490	$550
Realization vs Std Rate	88%	82%	80%	84%
Fees per Client	$1,100,000	$328,000	$29,333	$127,568
Direct Costs	$55,000,000	$48,000,000	$27,500,000	$130,500,000
Allocated Overhead Costs	$24,750,000	$21,600,000	$12,500,000	$58,850,000
Total Costs	$79,750,000	$69,600,000	$40,000,000	$189,350,000
Profit	$30,250,000	$12,400,000	$4,000,000	$46,650,000
Profit Margin % (vs Std)	24%	12%	7%	17%

Percentage	Large	Mid-sized	Small
Number of Clients	5%	14%	81%
Billable Hours Generated	42%	37%	21%
Fees @ Std Rates	45%	36%	20%
Fees Generated	47%	35%	19%
Profit	65%	27%	9%

Figure 3: High-level segmentation of the client base

This simple analysis provides some perspective on the firm's client base in terms of clients' consumption of firm resources and the corresponding profitability contribution of clients. As shown in the bottom table of this chart, the firm's clients form a pyramid whose base is made up of 80 percent of its clients who consume more than 20 percent of the firm's effort, but contribute less than 10 percent of the firm's profits. The top of the pyramid contains five percent of the firm's clients, but they contribute 65 percent of the firm's profit.

Design of the profitability model

The level of detail captured by and the design of VMH's profitability analysis system should be sufficient to at least produce the type of high-level analysis shown in the previous table, and to produce information on revenue and costs associated with each client.

If the firm has data such as industry classification or the area of practice (product designations) tagged to its matter records, this data can be further segmented by those attributes. VMH's profitability analysis will be much more useful to its decision-makers if the analysis can draw correlations to its profit contribution and certain client characteristics, such as:

- The client's industry;
- The level of the client's decision-makers with whom the firm has the strongest relationship (i.e. is the responsible partner's relationship with the client's general counsel, CEO, or owner, or is it with a mid-level manager or someone on the GC's team?);
- Length of client relationship with the firm;
- Client financial risk/stability; and
- Types and breadth of products purchased from the firm.

If VMH does not have a sufficient breakdown of its products, client industry, and other attributes that the firm believes would inform its analyses, and/or this data is not reflected in its profitability analysis system, Susan should at least consider (in the short term) associating these designations with a selected subset of the clients she wishes to analyze. This will be a bit of a manual effort, but can be accomplished over a smaller sample of clients. To build out its longer-term profitability analysis capabilities, the firm should then consider backfilling this data in its practice management or other central client/matter system for a larger set of clients as well as capturing this information through its new business intake process.

If the firm's data is not sufficiently broken down into products (areas of practice) at the matter level or by some level of phase or task for a matter, meeting the objective of the client and product profitability analysis to understand what drives the underlying costs will be difficult. Where this detail is not available – and even in cases where it is – the firm will need to resort to an analysis of time records. Of course, the better the quality of the narratives of those time records, the easier it will be to categorize them into the cost drivers that will inform this analysis. If a review of time records is required, I would suggest making the investment in one of several business intelligence software applications on the market that apply natural language processing algorithms to read time card narratives. These applications can not only enhance your profitability analysis capabilities, but can provide better data more quickly for planning and pricing matters and projects for clients.

Profitability analysis

Below is a simple illustration of how VMH might start its client profitability analysis once it has segmented its clients by size or revenue contribution. This illustration focuses on the top 20 clients for VMH in its "large£ client segment. Five metrics associated with the most recent annual period are extracted (if more meaningful, the data could be extracted for multiple periods and aggregated – whatever provides the best representation of the clients' consumption of firm resources and the associated revenue and profitability for the client). The metrics provided are:

- Potential fees – hours recorded valued at standard bill rates;
- Expected fee revenue – reflects the impact of client discounts, write-downs, and potential for not collecting accounts receivable or unbilled time;
- Expected realization percentage – the ratio of expected fee revenue to fees at standard rates;
- Profit margin – the expected fee revenue less the direct and indirect costs consumed by the client; and
- Profit margin percentage – the ratio of the profit margin to fees at standard rates.

	1	2	3	4	5
Client	Fees @ Std Rates	Expected Fee Revenue	Realization %	Profit Margin	Profit Margin %
A	$4,250,000	$3,750,000	88%	$950,000	22%
B	$3,450,000	$2,850,000	83%	$700,000	20%
C	$2,500,000	$2,000,000	80%	$475,000	19%
D	$2,300,000	$2,150,000	93%	$675,000	29%
E	$2,200,000	$2,100,000	95%	$725,000	33%
F	$1,900,000	$1,850,000	97%	$675,000	36%
G	$1,850,000	$1,700,000	92%	$325,000	18%
H	$1,750,000	$1,550,000	89%	$500,000	29%
I	$1,750,000	$1,500,000	86%	$425,000	24%
J	$1,450,000	$1,250,000	86%	$200,000	14%
K	$1,400,000	$1,100,000	79%	$125,000	9%
L	$1,325,000	$1,250,000	94%	$375,000	28%
M	$1,200,000	$1,050,000	88%	$300,000	25%
N	$1,125,000	$950,000	84%	$225,000	20%
O	$1,000,000	$990,000	99%	$400,000	40%
P	$975,000	$800,000	82%	$250,000	26%
Q	$960,000	$875,000	91%	$175,000	18%
R	$800,000	$725,000	91%	$100,000	13%
S	$800,000	$650,000	81%	$175,000	22%
T	$725,000	$700,000	97%	$75,000	10%

Figure 4: Top 20 client profitability metrics

The chart below compares the clients, ordered by potential fees, and with comparisons to expected fee revenue and profit margin.

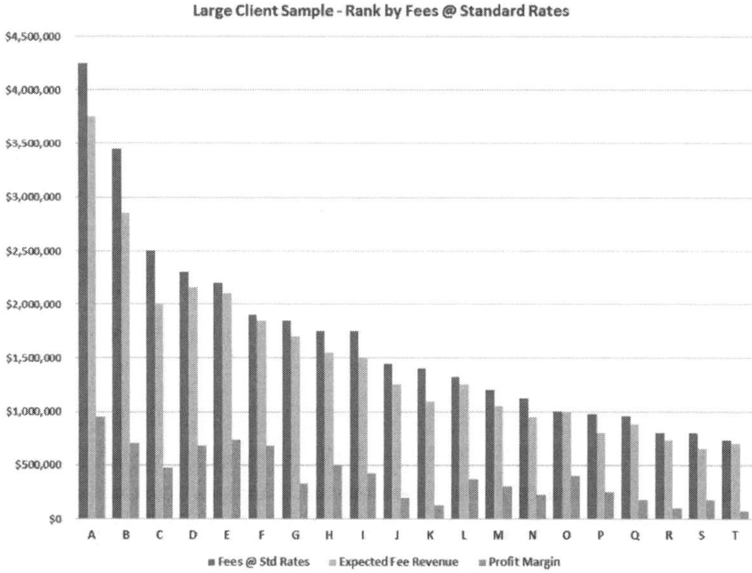

Figure 5: Client ranking by fees at standard rates

The second chart presents the clients by the amount of profit margin each contributes.

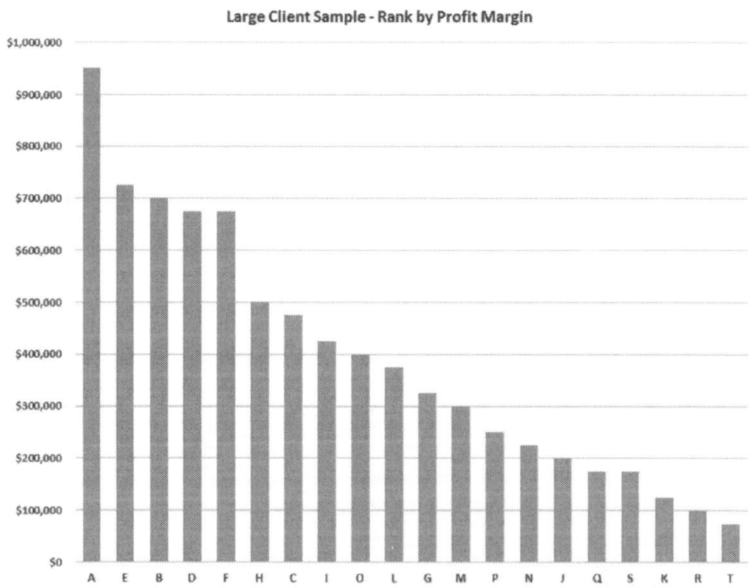

Figure 6: Client ranking by profit margin

This last chart ranks the 20 clients based on profit margin percentage.

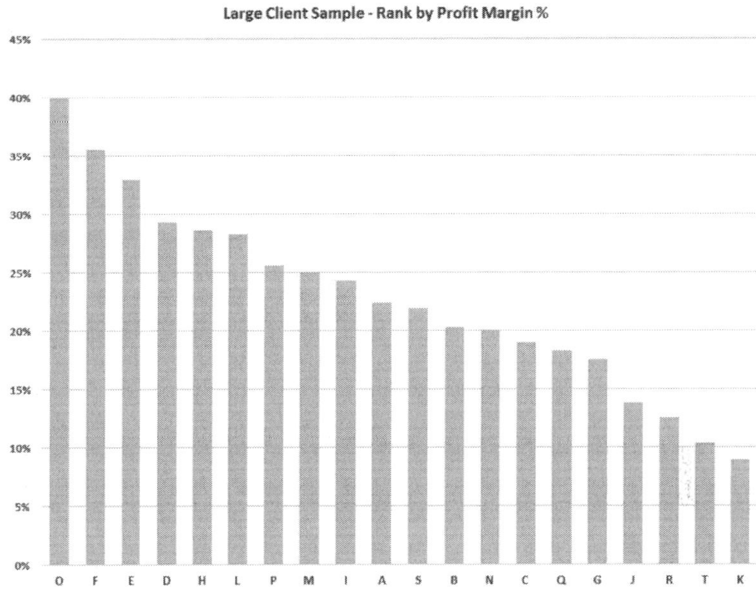

Figure 7: Client ranking by profit margin percentage

These simple charts provide some interesting information regarding some of the basic drivers of profitability within this segment of VMH's clients. You can begin to see which clients are carrying larger client discounts or are experiencing write-downs and other value adjustments, or which clients seem to absorb more resources and hence costs. These are all, of course, key clients for the firm, but also offer the greatest opportunity to make meaningful profitability improvements, adjust client retention and service strategies, or inform other profitability improvement opportunities across the firm's client portfolio.

Conclusion

This study of VMH provides a general framework and approach for undertaking a deep analysis of a firm's clients and products and segmenting those clients/products based on profitability and value to the firm. Identifying opportunities for redirecting resources to more profitable activities, and implementing cost management and revenue enhancement initiatives, is the intent of this analysis. Although the client and product profitability analysis process will provide VMH with a useful assessment of which clients and products are most profitable and which are not, the firm should carefully use this information when considering the value of the relationship with any client. Profitability alone may not be the only factor that gives a client value to the firm. An unprofitable client could provide sufficient value if it has the opportunity to provide future profitability growth, could lead to access or referral to other more profitable clients, strengthens the firm's presence in a certain market segment, is associated in a meaningful way with another key firm client or influencer, etc. Again, the observation that not all revenue contributes equally to profitability (or more broadly, value) has meaning in this sense.

VMH will be using their profitability analyses to identify where consumption of firm resources, and therefore cost, is misaligned with the revenues generated. Those observations may lead the firm to consider pursuing changes to its strategy, investments, procedures, and processes in order to improve profitability. It needs to be mindful that its cost structure will determine how overall results will be impacted by those changes. For example, if it is determined that less profitable or smaller clients will be transitioned to another firm, the costs historically associated with those clients will still exist. Unless those resources are redeployed to other revenue-producing (and profit-accretive) assignments, no cost has left VMH's operations. Likewise, VMH will need to consider how changes in strategy, procedure, and process will impact fixed overhead costs.

A well-designed and implemented client and product profitability model and the analysis it facilitates will provide the firm with valuable information on which it can take action. Further value can come from an extension of this historical-based analytical process to one that is prospective. The data developed from the historical-based process should provide the firm with the intelligence to project and model future revenue, cost and profit profiles for existing and potential clients, client segments and products.

Chapter 7:
Better business plans – a blueprint for strategy realization

By David Parnell, columnist and founder and principal of True North Partner Management

In 2017, my colleague Patrick McKenna and I surveyed 68 law firm leaders – mostly from AmLaw-ranked firms – about the planning, creation and subsequent execution of their firm-wide strategy. As we expected, most law firms had a strategy. In fact, only 2.9 percent of the responding firms "preferred to remain flexible and opportunistic", i.e., to have no formal plan. While the survey shed some light on several facets of the industry's position on strategy, most relevant to this chapter is the realization rate of the developed plans.

Importantly, when conducting our surveys, we are careful to avoid highly specific language, as doing so generally mitigates any potential anxiety or embarrassment that the answers in a multiple-choice format might cause. So, when we asked the respondents how much of their strategy was realized, the highest or best response was not identified as "ALL of the plan" but rather "ALMOST all of the plan." "Best", in our definition, is a *total* execution of the strategy. However, the language in the answers still allowed for some puffery: "almost" might represent 90 percent, 80 percent or even 60 percent of the plan, depending on how they perceived the question. Now, even when using the looser language, we found that only 3.2 percent of the firms executed at the highest response. In essence, the majority of firms are, as Patrick says, "seeing SPOTS", which is an acronym for "strategic plan on the shelf".

Taking a step back, one can speculate as to why these strategies go unexecuted; certainly, the reasons are myriad. That said, based on years of experience with lateral partners developing business plans and, throughout the process, seeing thresholds for acceptable business plans by the receiving firms, I am confident that firm-wide policies and processes that surround the creation of individual business plans are at least partly to blame.

Think about it: if your firm demands thorough, deep and up-to-date business plans and you decide to approach the lateral market, your business plan for a potential firm is – with a little bit of modification – already done upon market entry. This is rarely the case. Furthermore, if you are a law firm the demands thorough and deep business plans from your own partners, why would you accept anything less from a prospect? Again, based on my experience with the type and quantity of information that firms request from laterals, this often enough is not the case.

Strategies are highly important; especially when your firm does not have a +100-year-old, bullet-proof brand. However, that strategy is worthless if it's not put into action, which can only happen where the partnership has bought into it and each attorney has their own on-the-ground plan for attacking it.

An attorney's business plan is their map, their plan, their blueprint for the coming year. If it is done properly, it will fit inside the firm's strategy. It reacquaints the attorney with their current clients; it renews their interest in prospects; it forces a deeper familiarity with their markets; and it illustrates the web of resources and human capital that support and build their practice. With that in mind, let's look at some of the most important components of a thorough business plan, the benefits that each section can provide, and the many ways in which this process will better ensure that your firm does not see SPOTS.[1]

Firm-wide strategy

At the time of writing this chapter, I've interviewed 85 chairpersons/ managing partners from major firms for my *Forbes* column – close to 100 if you include practice heads – and in most instances, we discuss the firm's strategy. In addition, during the course of my search and placement work, I've spoken to many other law firm leaders and practice heads about strategy. Interestingly, over the years I've found that the market's grasp of all things strategy – what it is, an effective development process, the ability to succinctly describe it, mobilizing troops to execute it, etc. – sits on a vast spectrum. This can represent a problem for the firm in and of itself, certainly – if leadership doesn't understand their firm's strategy, how is the rest of the partnership to understand it?

While having your attorneys describe the firm's strategy in their business plan may seem *very* basic and redundant, it can be an illuminating barometer for firm leadership: do they actually get it? For a partner to function effectively as a gear in the strategy machine, they need to know what portion of the machine they are driving. There is no better way to ensure that than by asking them.

So, an effective business plan requires that the attorney understand the firm strategy – ideally putting it into their own words, if at all possible – and how, specifically, their practice fits into that business plan. Depending on the size of the firm, this will usually come in the form of a description of duties or responsibilities within the attorney's practice area. Working out that description consists of answering questions like: "What is the firm's current strategy? How will executing the strategy benefit you and your practice? How does your practice fit into that strategy? What could potentially happen to the firm should your practice group fail in its responsibilities within the strategy?"

This section comes first because it is the gateway through which all components of the business plan must pass. Doing this exercise forces the attorney to truly understand your firm's strategy, to make it their own by distilling it and putting it into their own words, and – perhaps most importantly – to really work through how their practice fits into it. The outcome of this process is (i) an overarching framework from which to decide upon and measure goals and activity moving forward, and (ii) a sense of the attorney's placement within the group and the firm as a whole.

See the following example:

> Our overarching strategy is to expand from our current regional to a national footprint by establishing Midwest and ultimately West Coast offices. This year, we are looking to start that process by creating an office in Chicago through the acquisition of an IP boutique. This will leverage our Boston- and DC-based clients' expressed needs in Chicago. We will ultimately seek to use the Chicago office as a springboard toward more national exposure.
>
> Many of the larger firms are buying up boutiques in this tighter legal market, and if we are to compete for the attractive firms, we'll need to be viewed as solid, brand-worthy and to have momentum. I know that our IP portfolio and transactional work, in particular, need to continue on with their upward trajectory if we are to remain an attractive acquirer in this market. It is therefore imperative that our IP group put together a plan that will keep the momentum going.
>
> If we are able to succeed with this, we'll have more work, more momentum, a better brand and, ultimately, a bigger pie from which to compensate all of us. If we fail, not only will that pie shrink, it could cost us an opportunity to move Westward; or worse, it could potentially have us acquiring a less-than-ideal boutique that could cause real cultural and economic issues down the road.

Practice summary

Of course, you'll want them to provide a practice summary. At a minimum, this should be the attorney's website biography, which will ideally provide an explanation of their practice from a 10K ft. view: what they do, the types of clients and matters that they support/engage, the markets they serve, and the general makeup of their client demographic. Please see the following example:

> While my clients come from a wide variety of industries and backgrounds, much of my experience is with manufacturing and engineering firms which serve the robotics and industrial sectors. My ideal clients are those middle market entrepreneurial businesses that populate the geographies of Washington, DC and VA.
>
> Clients typically have sales between $25 to $100M and maintain national footprints – often with international sales. I have also worked extensively with aerospace and defense contractors on general business, tax and M&A transactions. For example, I have several good referral sources within the aerospace and defense industry that have resulted in transactions for aerospace gear manufacturers, parts manufacturers and engineering services. As a result, I have made a concerted effort to understand the industry's different manufacturing tolerance levels, contract bidding processes and its financial modeling. In addition, I have also helped a number of clients in the professional practices, including several accounting firm acquisitions for a national accounting firm, mergers of several insurance brokerage firms, and the sale of several financial advisory firms.
>
> My geographic territory has around 350,000 privately owned businesses, many of which are in the lower half of the middle-market; the owners are generally 65+, many of which wanted to sell between 2008 and 2012 when values were depressed and sales dropped precipitously. Today, values are high and businesses now have experienced multiple years of increasing sales and healthy EBITDA margins. Private equity firms have been raising funds and their activity is increasing in pace. Their need to invest has caused many to move money at higher multiples and into smaller sized transactions. For example, I worked on three deals with out-of-state private equity buyers, all under $10M transaction value in the last couple of years. My expectation is the next 5 – 10 years will see significant turnover of the ownership of these companies and is an area that I believe will fit into our firm strategy.

Practice focus

Here, you'll want the attorney to be more specific about the actual breakdown of their practice composition. Be sure to include a full accounting of their practice and if possible (generalized) percentages of time consumed by each (e.g. 55 percent buy- and sell-side M&A; 25 percent public-private partnerships; etc.). I often find that attorney's label themselves as a particular type of attorney – "I'm an M&A attorney", for instance – despite the fact that that is only 50 percent of what they do on a daily basis and their skill set is more versatile. While they, of course, intuitively know what they do, the entire partnership may not. Having a deeper accounting of this can not only help the attorney to see where they are spending their time and areas that can potentially be leveraged for more work, but it can also help the firm's practice leadership see potential synergistic connections. Please see the following example:

I concentrate my practice in the following practice areas (note – the percentage next to each is my typical concentration based on hours worked in each area).

- **Mergers and acquisitions (60 percent)** – helping clients with formation, purchase, sale, reorganization, business succession planning, restructuring of the equity and capital of a business along with splitting up a business, buy-sell agreements, shareholder disputes and dissolutions. I work primarily with middle market entrepreneurial business owners. 70 percent of my M&A practice is sell-side and increasingly the buyers are out of state private equity firms or family offices.
- **Corporate, federal and state tax planning (15 percent)** – counsel on LLC operating agreements, contracts, tax structures, partnership and corporate shareholder tax planning, and structuring of tax appropriate incentive compensation alternatives. Tax structured planning and reorganizations used to be a significant part of my business but have receded over the last ten years as traditional M&A has increased.
- **Property tax appeals litigation (15 percent)** – representing commercial, industrial, retail, assisted and independent living centers and residential complexes in the appeal of their property tax values.

- **Corporate finance (five percent)** – bank loan documentation preparation and review, subordinated and mezzanine financing, recapitalization agreements, work-outs and forbearance agreements and private placement securities offering. Private placements are done with the assistance of securities counsel.
- **Nonprofit corporation representation (five percent)** – counsel and formation of new nonprofits, restructuring and revisions of bylaws and corporate records, mergers or dissolutions and application for, and compliance with, tax-exempt status for charitable, educational, religious and scientific organizations as well as nonprofit associations, trade groups, and social organizations.

Lawyer performance

Here, you are taking a deeper dive into the attorney's financials and stats. During lateral moves these numbers are almost universally requested because they are helpful for, among other things, illuminating any potential trends in the partner's production. To get a clear picture of that production generally requires at least three years of revenue, realization rates, billable hours, bill rates, leverage ratios and any consistent write-downs, discounts or write-offs. The latter, in particular, can be helpful in seeing any potential trends (particularly downward) in the attorney's client intake hygiene, the state of current client relationships, and/or attitudes/actions toward the administrative aspects of their responsibilities (i.e. financial hygiene).

Depending on the transparency of your firm's compensation model/process and your firm's attitudes toward compensation, it may also be helpful to include the attorney's compensation for each of the years in this section. The sum of the total can give you a "back of the napkin" view of what it looks like to finance the attorney's practice and whether any trends may be developing for a practice area or an individual attorney.

Please see the following example:

- Revenue: 2013 – $10.7M, 2014 – $10.4M, 2015 – $9.8M;
- Realization: 2013 – 95 percent, 2014 – 91 percent, 2015 – 82 percent;
- Write-downs/write-offs: – I do not offer significant or consistent write-downs for existing or new clients. 2015's lower realization is the result of several large bids that were lost;

- Hours worked and current bill rates: 2013 – 1,700/$1050; 2014 – 1,900/$1100; 2015 – 1,800/$1150; and
- Lawyer leverage – assuming partner-to-associate leverage of at least 3:1, it is reasonable to expect revenues in the range of $10-12M. The range is large because of the variables presented by lost deal discounts.[2]

Sector overview and opportunities

It is undeniable that an attorney's deep understanding of their client's industry is a highly sought-after commodity. In this section, the attorney is basically formalizing and crystallizing that sector knowledge. Much like the broad spectrum of the market's grasp on all things strategy, I've found there to be a broad spectrum of industry/sector knowledge where the practicing attorney is concerned. Of course, this will vary based on the composition of one's practice – e.g., a generalist versus a niche player – but the more an attorney knows about the sectors/industries that they serve, the better.

In an ideal world, the partner would create a white paper or dossier on their sectors/industries; this could include a description of the sector, the general demographics or market position of the actual clients, any trends that the sectors are seeing, opportunities and potential pitfalls and ideally how the sectors may be affected by prevailing economic conditions, among other things. The attorney's success or failure at completing this section can be very helpful to leadership that is making decisions about pitch teams, client managers, and to whom and where training and mentoring resources are allotted.

Please see the following example:

The US infrastructure sector – namely transportation, water, social, and power generation and distribution – has attracted significant attention across the world from US and internationally prominent private equity funds, pension and sovereign wealth funds, construction companies, developers and operators who are either investing in the US for the first time or capitalizing on their local platforms. There are three key drivers for this interest:

- The combination of the cumulative effect of (i) widespread deferred maintenance and (ii) historic under-investment in U.S. infrastructure. The American Society of Civil Engineers' most recent estimate as to the amount of investment required over the next five years in U.S. road and bridge assets alone is hundreds of billions of dollars. Further, fiscal distress at all levels of government is resulting in policy initiatives to drive alternative innovative procurement of significant, complex US infrastructure assets (i) at the federal level in the form of targeted finance programs intended to drive private investment in US infrastructure and technical assistance, and (ii) at the state and local level where many states and local governments have enacted public-private partnerships (P3) enabling legislation and are utilizing P3 as a means of delivering new infrastructure; e.g., roads, commuter and light rail systems, bridges, court houses and university campus redevelopments;
- The de-carbonization of distributed generation in the power sector will continue, creating opportunities for renewable energy project financings and secondary trades in operating assets; and
- Infrastructure is increasingly recognized as an asset class in its own right by pension systems, insurance companies, sovereign wealth funds and other long-term institutional investors. They are attracted to the non-cyclical and typically regulated, inflation-linked return profiles that the asset class offers. Institutional investors have increased allocations to this asset class over the last decade, and their investment activity, both directly and through their investments in infrastructure funds, has increased substantially. More specifically, aggregate funds under management have risen from $1.1B in 2004 to $317.5B by the end of 2014 (see: BlackRock – *Infrastructure Rising; An Asset Class Takes Shape* [2015]). Industry publications report unfeasible amounts of dry capital available and an eagerness to invest in energy and infrastructure. But even setting aside the hype, there is clearly a very substantial amount of investment capital, equity and debt, aggressively looking for opportunities.

Current clients

This is, by far, one of the most important sections of the plan. As we know quite well, the lifetime value of a client in the legal industry is extremely high – especially to the originating and/or relationship partner. So, without factoring in the many ways that cultural and practice norms can affect the ease with which partners share or covet their relationships, it is a safe bet that many don't just serve clients up to the partnership on a silver platter.

Why? Compensation models are usually the first place to look when client sharing isn't fluid and warm. However, the underlying values and attitudes that dictate how the compensation model works have usually been built into the firm's culture from the beginning. These aspects – the compensation model, the firm's culture and the group's psychology – are reciprocal, difficult to disentangle and are even more difficult to change. That said, to help overcome the coveting of relationships and files, a bit of pressure can be helpful, and having a firmwide client map will tell you exactly where to (gently and tactfully) apply that pressure.

Therefore, here, the attorney will lay out their current client list. Depending on the number of clients they have, it can be helpful to grade them (i) by revenue and/or (ii) by the strength and durability of the relationships. Have them include at least their top ten clients, or all of their clients if they have less. They should also provide a general description of the level and nature of their relationships, the age range of those relationships, how those relationships originated (i.e., under what conditions), and whether they think that those relationships could readily be expanded into other work.

Please see the following two examples:

A graded client list without descriptions:

I am privileged to have a strong and loyal client base that I've worked with for many years. For the purposes of this business plan, I rank them solely based on revenue projections derived from past performance. My relationships are generally at the GC/EVP/CEO level, derive from referrals or pre-existing personal/professional relationships, and none are less than five years old. Should you be interested, I can provide further information and/or discuss the nature of each relationship individually upon request.

1. First tier clients – based on an analysis of revenue generation in previous years, the following are my top ten clients in order of total revenue; each of these clients are expected to generate revenues of at least $500,000 this year: (1) Client A (2) Client B (3) Client C (4) Client D (5) Client E (6) Client F (7) Client G (8) Client H (9) Client I (10) Client J;
2. Second tier clients – based on an analysis of revenue generation in previous years, the following are my top 11–20 clients in order of total revenue, and each of these clients are expected to generate revenues of approximately $250,000 – $300,000 of revenue per year, not necessarily this coming year: (1) Client A (2) Client B (3) Client C (4) Client D (5) Client E (6) Client F (7) Client G (8) Client H (9) Client I (10) Client J; and

3. The following are my top ten clients by revenue generated for each of the last three years:
   a. 2013: (1) Client A (2) Client B (3) Client C (4) Client D (5) Client E (6) Client F (7) Client G (8) Client H (9) Client I (10) Client J;
   b. 2014: (1) Client A (2) Client B (3) Client C (4) Client D (5) Client E (6) Client F (7) Client G (8) Client H (9) Client I (10) Client J;
   c. 2015: (1) Client A (2) Client B (3) Client C (4) Client D (5) Client E (6) Client F (7) Client G (8) Client H (9) Client I (10) Client J.

An ungraded client list with descriptions:

Many of my current client projects are M&A transaction-based, with the client relationship either ending or going dormant following the close of the transaction (and any post-closing activity). As such, marketing and client development is a constant effort. My relationships are generally with the primary owner of the business and the vast majority of my clients are referrals from cultivated professional relationships.

The following are my five best client relationships.

- Entrepreneur. Helped client sell their multi-state engineering business for $105M in cash and stock. Relationship was a referral from a CPA firm (with which I have a six-year relationship). There were a few post-closing tax concerns and ongoing negotiations on employment, income and leases on real estate. After the sale, client has continued to purchase real estate, invest in various ventures, and perform tax and succession planning. Typical annual fees: $70,000 – $100,000;
- Business owner of a specialized machine shop in the process of selling the business. It is a smaller firm at around $30M in revenue. He required assistance in seeking a buyer, preparing the company for sale, and will ultimately represent he and his company during the sale. The client was a referral from an attorney at another, smaller firm that represents the client's smaller family matters. Fee for the projects so far: $80,000 – $120,000;
- Business owner of a commercial aircraft business with ten different aircraft seeking to exit. This has been a client for six years and a referral from client #1 (entrepreneur). The process is just starting and the scope is not yet defined. Depending on the scope and whether an investment bank is hired, or if I assist with the location of a buyer, fees will range: $50,000 – $150,000;

- Real estate investor. The client owns several real estate ventures, including hotels and is a referral from my networking group. I am assisting them with a new development project including property tax abatements and possibly brownfield redevelopment. Real estate counsel will be needed to assist. Fee estimate: $35,000 – $70,000, depending on how the project progresses;
- Private equity firm seeking a lower-end middle market buyer. I found this contact via LinkedIn research. The fee is based upon an alternative model with a contingent fee based upon a closing. Fee estimate: $100,000 – $150,000 once target is acquired; and
- Beyond the foregoing, I have a list of 25 – 30 smaller clients whose fees are typically in the $5,000–$7,500 range, and other clients who are not currently active but for whom I remain in contact and ready to assist in their next legal need. These include an industrial tire manufacturer, an engineering staffing agency, a home health care agency, several smaller tool or product manufacturers, several individual or smaller investment firms, several smaller nonprofit entities, inventors and several clients who I helped to sell their business and that are now employees of their buyers. I also have 10–15 estate planning clients, most of whom are business owners or investors. I do not draft estate plans but I target estate planning clients as easier entries into the relationship.

Target clients

Following the previous section will be any clients that are immediately-approachable or realistically approachable in the next six to 12 months. Potential clients beyond this time frame are generally too prospective for the scope of this section and can be addressed in the marketing section. Your attorneys should be careful not to forget those clients that they've avoided and/or lost because of conflicts, lack of support practices, etc. Firm conditions, practice portfolios, geographic footprints and firmwide client lists can change without the attorney's knowledge, which may create potential opportunities.

A boon to this section can be leadership gaining a better understanding of the attorney's client intake hygiene. Does there appear to be a focus on a particular client type or client caliber? Is there brand-building value to the client bands the attorney is aiming for? While it is important for the attorney to have a good idea as to the base that they are going after – a primary purpose of this section – it is also important to manage the overall value of those clients, i.e., future introductions that they might make; the brand-building signals sent to the market; the impact their general payment terms may have on profitability; etc. This section can help immensely with this.

Please see the following example:

> I do not focus heavily on direct marketing of target clients, but instead focus on building strong personal relationships with referral sources that can provide multiple client opportunities per year. However, I do maintain a few targets that I have relationships with but haven't landed due to conflicts, timing or missed opportunities because of deficiencies in our current practice portfolio. While none of these are imminent clients, all are active targets who I strongly believe would be realistic activations with a bit of tweaking and/or the right mix of a pitch team and support:
>
> (a) A China-based electronics manufacturer that has been looking to acquire real estate for expansion and investment, State-side;
>
> (b) A large nonprofit who is developing real estate around the Austin and Dallas areas using various tax incentives and LITCs;
>
> (c) An out of state M&A investor who is looking for companies to acquire for their portfolio;
>
> (d) A Michigan-based trucking company that I have a relationship with and a strong outside champion referral source, but with whom our firm has had an ongoing conflict;
>
> (e) A defense general contractor who expressed reservations due to lack of government contracting experience; and
>
> (f) An engineering services firm with which I have maintained contact due to my experience in the industry, and that I have heard is looking to sell in the near future. I also have a relationship with a possible acquirer.
>
> I also actively target old clients that I have not worked with recently, including an industrial tire manufacturer; a home health care business seeking to expand; an engineering staffing firm that expressed a desire to sell a few years ago but that I had to refer a litigation piece out due to a conflict; and a foundry that either needs to grow or sell in the near future.

Marketing strategy and practice development

At a 5K ft. view, how will the attorney seek to acquire and grow their targets and any other unspecified prospective clients? It is one thing to know who those targets are; it is another thing to have a plan for acquiring them. What in-roads do they have? What affiliations can they leverage? What practices might hunt with them to acquire the business?

How are they going to market themselves and the firm? Are they actively building a brand? If so, how?

In addition, are there any plans to further develop their legal and/or business skills? Are they considering further education or professional development coursework or coaching? This type of information can be helpful to each practice group leader when considering whether and how the marketing plans fit into the firm's overall strategy, and where firm-based marketing and training resources will be allotted.

Please see the following example:

> Most of my marketing activities are conducted on my own, as our firm engages in little firm-wide marketing or branding efforts. I have therefore initiated an M&A practice group that is centered on marketing, which I informally lead. I have started to arrange bi-monthly mixers with our transactional attorneys and various accounting firms, investment banks, commercial banks, and financial planning firms. The goal is to increase strategic relationships and increase brand awareness.
>
> From a content standpoint, my goal is to write and publish marketing articles or give client presentations throughout the year. Articles have covered tax appeals, M&A transactions, nonprofits and similar topics.
>
> The vast majority of my clients are from referrals which I have strategically cultivated over the years. I have created a strong list of referral partners that is heavy with investment bankers, PE firms, accounting firms, financial planning firms, real estate brokers and other professionals. I therefore started an independent networking group which currently has 14 professionals from different disciplines that meets twice per week and which hosts 6–8 social gatherings per year. This group is responsible for several of my current top ten clients.
>
> Lastly, I find that my clients are increasingly coming to me for business advice as opposed to just legal advice, which I believe is the pathway to becoming a "trusted advisor". So as to be of stronger value to them and ideally facilitate this process, I will be attending several regional and national industry events this year.

Prospecting and client development

Here, we are getting into the on-the-ground, nitty-gritty of how the attorney plans on actually attacking the market. The depth and specificity of this section will (or should) depend on the attorney's maturity as a practitioner. In the case of a more junior partner who doesn't have a large, diversified and well-aged book, this section should be a bit more robust and specific in nature. It should essentially be a mini-marketing plan, including things like: mining existing contacts, creating new relationships (internally and externally), cross-marketing with specific firm clients, writing articles/blogs/books, speaking on panels, joining industry groups, participating on boards, community involvement, leveraging video and/or social media; frequenting events and groups that harbor potential clients; tracking mentions of potential clients in the press and then contacting them; etc. Further, and importantly, it is advisable to have specific, trackable activity goals. Where business development is concerned, daily/weekly activity is the single aspect that the attorney does have control over, and the law of averages dictates that when the numbers are achieved, the business follows.

Please see the following examples:

Junior partner

For the last year-and-a-half, I have worked with a sales coach and training program to help increase my capability for prospecting and qualifying leads, dealing with price objections, increasing efficiency and increasing closing rates on opportunities. Throughout this process, I have narrowed down a sale and prospecting system to track my annual, monthly, weekly and daily minimum sales and marketing efforts that are needed to reach my desired goals.

My near-term goals for the next 12–18 months built up from a TTM (trailing twelve months) average are $700,000 in working receipts and $500,000 in origination receipts, $50,000 – $100,000 of which would be performed by other attorneys. My long-term originations goal (three to five years) is $1M. While, of course, I cannot guarantee the ultimate outcome, my experience has been that by focusing on and achieving the activity goals, the numbers will follow. In order to achieve those results, I have created the following workflow:

- $500,000 originations / $400,000 typically recurring = $100,000 new needed;
- New clients needed this year – four at avg. $25,000 in fees each;
- Eight client opportunities needed at a 50 percent closing rate;
- and 35 significant conversations needed to generate eight to 10 opportunities;
- Generating opportunities:
    - Five calls to new contacts/sources/clients/old clients each day;
    - Provide two referrals to sources each week;

- Ask for two referrals from sources and clients each week;
- Two to three lunch/breakfast/coffee meetings with sources each week;
- Four networking/prospecting events per month (ACG/chambers/CFA/SEM);
- Five new quality contacts per event/five touches to existing contacts;
- One article or seminar every other month;
- Avg. five LinkedIn contacts or new connections per week; and
- Biannual direct mailings for property tax/succession planning.

The senior partner will need not be as in-depth – assuming that they are already successful. Please see the following example:

Senior rainmaker

Marketing – activities to raise the profile of the firm and practice in the market.

- I am a frequent sponsor of, and speaker at, industry conferences, which has been an effective way to raise and maintain a high profile if done selectively where sponsorship is not saturated by legal competitors;
- I have hosted an annual industry client event for the last eight years which usually attracts around 100 of my New York-based contacts and has become a fixture on clients' calendars;
- I regularly participate in industry policy discussions and see value in convening thought leadership-oriented dinner series with senior clients and public officials; and
- "INDUSTRY GATHERING" has been an effective profile booster for me and can be leveraged to raise the firm's profile in the infrastructure industry as well as the profiles of other members of the firm who can be encouraged to participate and network.

Synergies with other practices

I've found "synergistic" practice groups to be a highly sought-after commodity to most, if not all, attorneys. All firms tout this characteristic, but just saying it doesn't make it so; there is often quite a bit of work that goes into achieving it. Certainly, an aspect of creating a synergistic environment is having a broader understanding of which of the firm's attorneys need help, what kind of help they need, from which practices they need that help, and ideally from which attorneys they need that help from.

Now, "help" is a big word; it can mean practice support, pitch support, mentorship, leverage, or more. For leadership to know these things is immensely helpful in their planning, and the best way to get it is to ask. Therefore, here, the attorneys will be answering questions like: "Which practice groups do you believe will help your practice? From which ones will you want pitch partners to come from? With your current network within the firm, who are you *really* working with? Are there existing synergies that work?"

The street goes both ways: "What practice groups do you expect *your* practice to help at our firm? What clients do you have currently that can be mined for more work outside of your practice area? Can you offer mentorship to a younger attorney? Would you be interested in helping to train others on the business aspects of your industry?"

Lastly, your attorneys shouldn't expect firm leadership to *completely* drive this aspect of the firm's business model. It is therefore appropriate to ask: "How will you go about expanding and fostering the development of these synergies and relationships?"

This section will essentially describe what types of relationships they currently have, what relationships they'd like to have, and what they are willing to do in order to get from point A to point B.

Please see the following example:

- M&A Transactions. M&A is my area of practice strength and will remain my primary focus; my main client base for future growth is going to continue being the institutional investor market. I have strong relationships with fund managers and institutional investors on the transactional side which I can leverage to help feed our fund formation practice. Further, my strong mid-market experience is something that some of our large-cap clients might be able to use should they decide to branch into the market of smaller funds.
- Portfolio company work. This includes general corporate, litigation, and restructuring work, all of which can be pitched for from my existing client base by our respective practices. We've done a bit of cross-selling in the past, but we've not nearly exhausted the opportunities. In essence, each deal I do for my PE clients creates a potential corporate client for the firm, and these clients can spin off significant corporate, restructuring, regulatory, and litigation work.

- I also have a growing client base in the project finance and energy and infrastructure sectors that can provide a natural synergy with our high profile real estate practice – in particular for transactions structured as "hybrids" with both real estate and infrastructure sector features.
- Property tax appeals. This is an area that will be ripe to expand in the next couple of years when real estate values correct following the recent surge. Much of this work can be handed down to younger associates and staff and often has contingent fee payments well in excess of multiples of the hourly rates invested.

Below is how I might envision developing new synergies:

I will need to more thoroughly assess our team's current knowledge/skills base to determine where training might be needed. This might start with a better understanding of the resources available in each practice group, the dynamics between each group and even inner-group etiquette. To date, I have only very loosely evaluated these areas. With leadership's help, I will seek to establish a much more formalized understanding of these areas.

I plan on doing this by establishing personal contact with as many partners as possible – priority being those that will most directly impact my six-month business plan and whose business I can immediately impact. This way I can determine who is interested in (and is in a position to) benefit from my expertise and the relationships that I currently have in the market. Importantly, I will proactively seek to create open channels of communication and to begin working on interpersonal relationships with them.

Once semiformal-to-formal pitch teams have been established – i.e., I've gained mutual interest and agreement – I will systematically meet with the team/s to cooperatively develop a hunting plan for our group. This will include creating prioritized lists of clients to go after, a general plan of how I will go after them, and creating "receivables" that each member will be responsible for and held accountable to.

As quickly as possible, I will commence introducing the various partners to my current clients in an effort to better institutionalize them, to build more business, and otherwise support the development of the business and the firm.

Required resources

Here, the attorney is discussing the team and firm resources that their practice will need so as to ultimately be successful. General areas to be addressed might be support required from other practices – dovetailing from the prior section – technology, marketing, skill and knowledge base development (including legal, sectoral and professional), and/or other personal needs (such as time off).

Possible questions to be answered: "What types and how many supporting attorneys will you need to continue servicing your clients at acceptable-to-stellar rates? What other practices are necessary to fully support your clients? What other practices in our firm could pitch to your existing clients for more work? What is necessary for you to realize your marketing efforts? What are your thoughts on creating formalized hunting packs for business development? Is there a particular technology that will be helpful to you or that your clients have requested?"

Answering questions like these (and more) will allow you (leadership) to make educated decisions about what, if anything, will be necessary to ensure that the attorney's plan – and therefore, the firm's strategy – is successful.

Please see the following example:

> Some of my biggest current challenges could become strengths with the potential modifications that our current strategy is aiming to achieve.
>
> - Practice depth. Unfortunately, I've lost some large and attractive client opportunities, and referral sources have passed on forwarding a significant project to me, because of the perceived lack of depth in our current M&A and leveraged finance practices. Because of this, in the recent past, I have not spent significant time chasing a number of specific clients because I am confident that they would not regard us as viable. Our focus on recruiting into our current M&A practice – in San Francisco, in particular – is exciting. Some other areas that I would love to see expanded in the future would be SAR/ITAR/ contracting for defense and aerospace clients, tax incentives for developers, and deeper regulatory/compliance capabilities for larger national and international M&A transactions.
> - Marketing strength. While I am very active in marketing and networking, personally, and have been able to get some of my partners to start being involved in regular "mixer" events, the lack of general marketing investment makes my task significantly more difficult. It just isn't a part of the culture, here. The ability to access

more strength in marketing, including development on marketing materials, industry and practice area knowledge and increased sponsorships and advertising will help me take sales for new clients to a new level.

- Lastly, I currently lack material access to younger talented attorneys who can work more efficiently on projects. For better or worse, our financial model is not very conducive to retaining quality young associates – as you likely know from several key departures this past year – and as such I have far too few to support client growth. Being able to leverage skilled younger associates will help increase my efficiency.

Discussion and analysis

This is the final section and is a catchall of sorts. It is likely that in having finished an entire business plan of this caliber, the attorney will have some new and other ideas, concerns or considerations otherwise and will need a place to reveal those to firm leadership. Does the attorney have anything else that they'd like to discuss? Are there any observations about the above information that are important and relevant? Are there any projections that may be helpful? Here is the place to discuss it.

Please see the following example:

Numbers. While I have only provided the practice numbers for the past three years (2014-2016), they are generally consistent with previous years of production and what I expect for 2017; although a significant improvement in the amount of revenue and realization over 2015 is reasonable to expect. 2015 was an aberration in terms of write-offs for deals lost by clients in an aggressive bidding market. This is the nature of the private equity industry at this point and as long as our clients continue to bid – which they will – the law of averages will level this out. I am happy to discuss this further.

Predicting deal flow. It is notoriously difficult to forecast M&A deal flow with any precision. But based on current trends in M&A and prevailing macroeconomic conditions, I expect to see a bias towards M&A this upcoming year. While many first (and even second) generation infrastructure funds are exiting investments, sell-side conditions are favorable with low interest rates and a multitude of investors with dry powder.

Recruitment/team. Successfully competing in the industries I represent requires a broad set of legal and industry-relevant skills. Lawyers on the team need to be trained on corporate transactional structures and documentation, finance and security documentation (including the private placement market and government funding programs), as well as lease and concession documentation, construction contracts, and other commercial contracts. Sector knowledge is critical to my success as it enables me to perceptually and practically differentiate our firm from firms that otherwise possess strong private equity or project finance practices but are lacking in-depth knowledge of the assets being bought or sold or financed.

My experience. My experience and background have always been in working with high-energy clients. Many times, these can be difficult personalities that move at a fast pace, demand quick answers, and fight like a bulldog in negotiations. Having worked with two mentors who were similar personalities, I've learned how to not only handle these clients but also to thrive with them. Experience tells me that, while they are challenging, they also tend to pay well and pay quickly, if you can build a good relationship with them. I am happy to share any of my experience and/or knowledge with my partners that may be having challenges with this same type of client.

Conclusion

Try not to get sticker shock when you're considering the size and girth and, therefore, work that goes into a business plan like this. Of course, you will need to modify this to fit into the general appetite of your firm's partnership. However, don't let this acknowledgment become an "out" for you to avoid applying some pressure on your partners. In the event that there is considerable pushback, I encourage you to do your own pushing for as much completion of this plan from your partnership as possible, with the idea that the more you can get the better off the firm will be.

An exercise like this is analogous to sharpening a dull or damaged knife. There is a significant amount of work, time and even skill necessary in the upfront process, but once the blade is sharpened – i.e., the first business plan has been created – it only needs to be tuned up every so often; the entire process does not need to be done again and again.

Lastly, it will be helpful to take a long-term approach. In the event that there is pushback, at least start the process of creating an in-depth plan like this with junior/recently initiated partners – chalk it up as just another part of their responsibilities. Just like any other shift in your firm's business model, it needs to start somewhere. Consistency over time will ultimately integrate this process into the general flow and culture of the firm.

Reference

1. Note: the following examples are from various business plans I've worked with over the years – M&A, private equity, project finance, infrastructure, IP, etc. – and some of the information has been changed to ensure confidentiality. This is not to be representative of a single, fluid business plan.

Chapter 8: Insourcing and its commercial attractiveness in boosting profitability

By Srinivas Vadali, principal management consultant at PA Consulting, and Manish Khandelwal, IT transformation expert at PA Consulting

Insourcing is on the rise

Outsourcing has brought significant benefits to many organizations. It has delivered real cost savings and improvements in quality across many different sectors. Outsourcing companies have become more sophisticated and offer a wider range of services to high standards. However, in today's increasingly complex and fast-changing business environment, it is clear that companies now need to review their outsourcing decisions and explore whether alternative sourcing options offer better ways to drive the next phase of cost reduction and quality improvements.

One of those options is insourcing, through which companies bring certain components of their IT and shared services in-house and rebalance their capability supply chain. The trend is to look for a better balance between building capability and buying it by using both insourcing and outsourcing options effectively. In our experience, by including insourcing in the mix, organizations can establish a scalable platform that achieves significant ongoing cost reduction, improves business integration, and fosters innovation.

Insourcing helps to retain the critical knowledge in-house, enables agile project delivery, and helps to identify opportunities for automation. These advantages then give organizations much greater agility to respond to changes in demand, both in their marketplace and within their businesses. As companies look to improve customer centricity, insourcing gives them greater flexibility to meet the customer needs.

As the potential benefits of insourcing have become clearer, we have seen growing interest and willingness among business leaders to consider a wider range of sourcing options. The 2017 UK IT Outsourcing Study, conducted by Whitelane Research in collaboration with PA Consulting Group, found that while there was still an appetite for outsourcing, 22 percent of IT services clients said that they now plan to outsource less. The same proportion (22 percent) said they saw outsourcing as a barrier to increased agility. There is also evidence that a number of companies are recognizing that in some areas, where business knowledge and proximity are key, insourcing can offer real benefits.

There are significant potential cost savings from insourcing

In recent decades, when driving out inefficiencies was critical to business success and even survival, outsourcing became popular because of the opportunity it brought to reduce operating costs. For many companies, that decision has proved highly effective and their outsourcing contracts have delivered significant savings.

However, it has always been necessary to weigh up the advantages of outsourcing against the downsides. This is particularly true in today's business climate, where flexibility and responsiveness are increasingly important success factors. Outsourced services with restrictive contracts can make it hard for companies to respond in an agile way to a fast-changing marketplace. They can also stifle innovation as the contractor focuses on providing the services they are contracted to supply.

Most business decisions still come down to cost, but here again some companies are finding that outsourcing is not always the most cost-effective option. A number of organizations have discovered that when they bring services back in-house, even with already outsourced/offshored services, it gives them an opportunity to further reduce the same cost base.

While the common perception is that the insourced operations are more expensive than outsourced ones, our experience with a range of clients suggests that if insourcing is managed effectively, organizations can secure cost savings in the range of 20-50 percent, depending on the scope, where they are in the overall development of their business, and their target operating model.

There are a number of ways in which savings can be achieved through insourcing. The full range of potential savings are:

Lower end of the savings range – (a) organizations that have outsourced and offshored. Savings at this end of the range can be achieved by organizations that have already outsourced their IT and shared services delivery to a third-party supplier in low-cost locations. They should be able to reduce their operating costs by a further 20 percent when they insource the service delivery to low cost offshore locations.

In an outsourced situation, the client's perception of cost is usually different from the total cost of the service consumption through a third-party supplier. This total cost will be higher than the vendors' rates by as much as 20 percent when VAT and IT overheads are included. Also, even if there is an assumption that the client has negotiated a good deal with their current service provider or even re-negotiated the contract with the incumbent or a new service provider, the fully loaded cost the supplier will charge will include the vendor's profit margin,[1] which will be about 20 percent.

In contrast, when a company runs the operation themselves in an offshore location, they will be able to save on the vendor margins and vendor overheads. Further, higher levels of offshoring are achievable for an insourced outfit, leading to additional gains.

Higher end of savings range – (b) organizations with current footprint largely in high-cost locations. The potential savings will be much higher for organizations that currently run most of their IT and business support functions in high-cost onsite locations. They can achieve savings of up to 50 percent in operating expenditure through offshoring the operations to a low-cost location, while still keeping the operations in-house.

With labor costs in low-cost locations about 55-65 percent lower than those in higher cost ones, companies moving their services offshore will see their existing costs reduce by up to half, after factoring in staff, building and facilities overheads. That can provide a cost reduction of about 35 percent of current operating expenditure.

Moreover, a further saving of about 15 percent on these ranges is usually achievable if companies implement a transformation plan which is focused on securing the synergies of the captive center as it matures the way it delivers services. In particular, moving to a model which is much more focused on the outcomes of the delivery teams will drive further efficiencies.

Busting misconceptions about insourcing

Despite these advantages, many business leaders have been cautious about going down the insourcing route. The reluctance stems partly from the many myths about the costs of setting up and running insourced operations, which have created a view that they are more expensive than they really are. The concerns and questions which are holding companies back from making the decision to insource are:

- Is there a huge upfront cost?
- Do I need high volumes (500 or 1,000 people) to make a strong case and make it sustainable?
- What is the payback period? and
- Is there a long lead time?

In our experience, the answers to these questions should provide some reassurance that insourcing projects can be manageable and cost effective. In our work, we have seen examples where even when roles are already outsourced to offshore locations and the numbers of people involved are as low as 100, a strong business case for insourcing can be made.

While there will be upfront costs, insourcing projects can provide a return on investment much in excess of industry standard of 12 percent, a multi-million net present value (NPV) and payback in about three years. Equally, it does not have to take a long time to get the new approach in place. With right set of delivery capabilities and leadership, the lead time in setting up an insourcing operation can be as short as 12 months.

There is growing evidence that, when insourcing is done right, it offers a very attractive commercial proposition as well as real qualitative benefits through increased control and improved synergies.

How insourcing works in practice

PA has been working with various clients to help them re-balance their capability supply chain and introduce a variety of sourcing solutions. Our clients typically face increasing demands from the businesses for better control over its IT delivery and a strong desire to make better use of its existing assets, in addition to meeting a significant cost reduction target. This means that they invariably need to re-asses their global delivery strategy and how they provide services to the business.

There are multiple challenges to overcome in these engagements, not least the organization's dependency on outsourced partners. Further problems can then arise if the service delivery organization is misaligned with the overall strategy and so has a lack of control and ownership. Location footprint and spread out assets can also prove challenging. All these create a clear case to look at doing things differently.

In response, it is best to develop and shape a sourcing strategy along with a location strategy to address these problems. Insourcing operations can provide solutions to these problems, underpinned by a strong business case that has potential to offer a multi-million NPV saving and up to a 50 percent reduction in operating expenses, depending on the scope, location and target operating model.

Once the business case is well understood, a transformation program must be built to drive the establishment of an in-house capability to deliver IT and shared services at the selected location. Once the service center is set up, multiple services can be transitioned within a span of 12 months.

Once the capability is established, it can be scaled up to keep up with continued margin pressures to deliver additional savings. Our experience of completed captive centers and the business cases for those in-flight indicate that potential net savings of up to 40 percent can be achieved when the client moves service delivery to offshore and near-shore locations. What is critical to achieving those savings is getting the right location for the captive center to ensure that it can comfortably secure the skills needed at a competitive cost.

Key considerations

While the benefits of insourcing are increasingly clearer, before they make a decision to go down this route, organizations do need to have a very clear understanding of their needs. That should start with a review of their current global delivery and sourcing strategy. This should include a qualitative and quantitative assessment of the full range of possible options. This can then be used to inform the creation of a high-level business case that can reshape the sourcing strategy.

In all this work it is important to be open to all the possibilities. For one of our clients, we assessed ten different sourcing options (insource, outsource, build-operate-transfer etc.) against sixteen strategic parameters in order to develop a recommendation for the final option. This comprehensive and open approach is the best way to ensure that the business can make a fully informed decision about what will work for them.

It is critical to draw up a detailed business case and benefits realization plan. This should include an analysis of the current operating model, potential demand and target location strategy. It is particularly important to get the location strategy right. The location will be critical to securing the desired savings, quality of services and scalability of the center. That means careful research needs to be undertaken to ensure that the location provides good access to the talent that will be needed and that the relevant services and skills can be secured at a competitive cost.

There is no one solution that will fit every company and it is important to develop a strategy that is tailored to the needs of each organization. However, our experience shows that, for many organizations, increasing the insourced to outsourced ratio will improve the likelihood of achieving their business objectives. It will provide a clear means to achieve the cost reductions and increased control that will give them the flexibility to manage today's business challenges more effectively.

Reference

1. Top four Indian outsourcer operating profit margin in 2015 ranges from ~18–27 percent (Source: BNP Paribas, Mint Research, http://www.livemint.com/Companies/Vnh7s3UKmKHpmJlg5rcrnK/Profits-take-a-back-seat-for-Indian-IT-firms.html).

Chapter 9:
A model to gauge and understand fee-earners' performance

By Rupert Hawke, managing director of UK firm Cartwright King

An illustrative approach

A large sheet of fee-earner performance numbers prepared by your accounts team can be challenging to tackle and decipher as a manager. Making the issues understood by fee-earners can also prove difficult. After all, it might be argued there is a negative correlation between an enthusiasm for accountancy and the law!

A simple illustrative approach that shows performance based on two key factors is helpful to both the manager and fee-earner. Importantly, it provides clues to why a fee-earner is deviating from the expectation, which in turn can contribute to effective management for that fee-earner.

The Boston Matrix was a marketing concept developed in the 1970s to plot where a business' product sat in terms of two variables: market share and market growth.

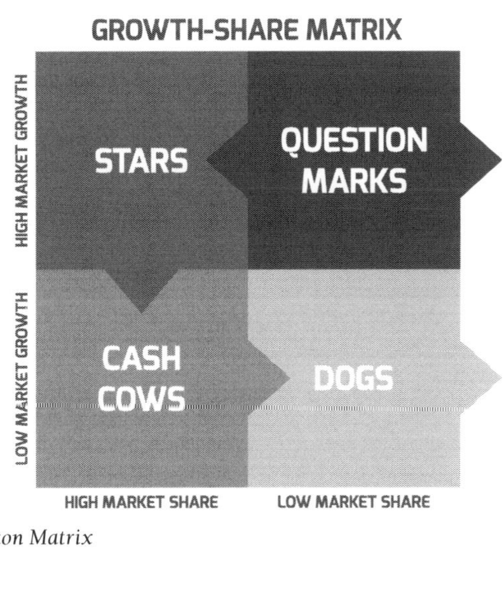

Figure 1: The Boston Matrix

Obviously, the more products in the top left corner and the fewer in the bottom right hand corner, the better! Once it is known which box a product sits in, a strategy can then be devised. For example, once a product is identified as a "question mark" with low market share and high market growth (top right hand box), it is likely to benefit from a strategy based on increasing the presense in the market place. Identifying a "star" (high market share/high market growth) will lead a business to look at developing similar products that could fit those criteria. And once a "dog" is identified (low market share/low market growth) it might make commercial sense to cease that offering as it is diluting the offerings of better performing products in the other three boxes.

Applying the Boston Matrix to fee-earner performance

The Boston Matrix concept of identifying two key factors that in turn allow for relevant strategies to be put in place can helpfully be applied to the fee-earning performance of a staff member in a law firm.

Instead of measuring market share and market growth, we measure two important factors for a fee-earner:

- Contribution (profit); and
- Time recorded.

Fees have been the traditional way of measuring fee-earner performance, but what is critical is whether the fee-earner makes an overall contribution (profit). It is reasonably simple to calculate the hourly return required by a fee-earner to break even (how much a fee-earner needs to make assuming they hit their chargeable hours target). The firm's annual central overhead budgeted costs (central staff, rent and rates, stationary, IT, etc) should be divided across all fee-earners (based on expected chargeable hours); this cost should be added to the fee-earner's salary cost (including the employer's social security and pension contributions). This total figure should then be divided by the annual chargeable hours budget to get a break even return for that fee-earner.

Costing a fee-earner

Two examples (one full-time and one part-time employee) of how to arrive at a "cost per hour" for a fee-earner are below (assuming a f/t fee-earner is required to do 35 chargeable hours per week and there are six weeks' holiday per year):

Total central overheads	$2,100,000
Full time equivalent (FTE) fee-earners	75
Overhead allocated per FTE	$28,000

FEE EARNER 1: Full-time (35 hours PW)	
Salary (inc. social security & employer pension)	$54,000
Overhead allocated	$28,000
Total cost	$82,000
Annual chargeable hours budget	
(35 hours * 46 weeks)	1,610
Hourly break-even (cost per hour):	$50.93

FEE EARNER 2: Part-time (21 hours PW)	
Salary (inc. social security & employer pension)	$34,800
Overhead allocated (60% of FTE)	$16,800
Total cost	$51,600
Annual chargeable hours budget	
(35 hours * 27.6 weeks)	966
Hourly break-even (cost per hour):	$53.42

Figure 2: A cost per hour example

If a firm required a 20 percent return on the fee-earner costs, the above examples would have to make per hour:

Fee-earner 1: $50.93 * 120% = $61.12
Fee-earner 2: $53.42 * 120% = $64.10

If the fee-earner makes that return per hour and undertakes the hours set, they will then hit their target. However, if there are variations either in return per hour or time recorded, the position on the Boston Matrix will then give clues as to the reasons in variation against standard (above or below).

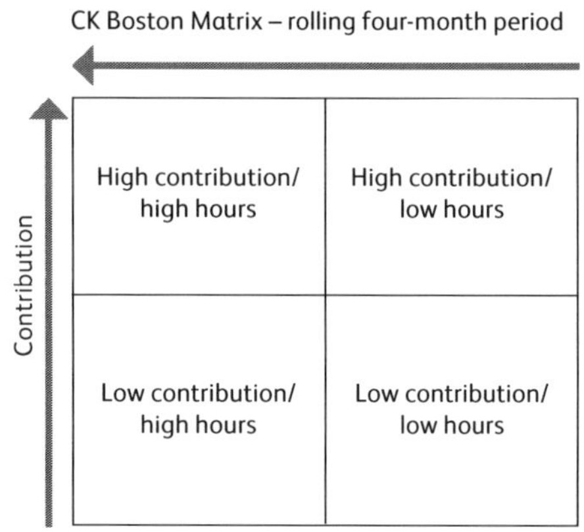

Figure 3: The Boston Matrix – a legal application

The box a fee-earner sits depends on the two variables discussed as follows:

- High contribution/high hours – undertakes a lot of work that provides good margin and/or is done efficiently – the box to aspire to be in;
- High contribution/low hours – undertakes good margin work and/or works efficiently but might not have enough work to do;
- Low contribution/high hours – undertaking work that does not provide enough margin and/or is overworking files – possibly working hard but not covering enough case work; and
- Low contribution/low hours – working inefficiently or on work that does not provide enough margin and is not undertaking enough work.

The aim is to get as many fee-earners into the top left-hand corner as possible! It is advisable to measure people over more than just one month to iron out any short-term anomalies like holidays. A four-month rolling basis can work well for gauging progress.

It is simpler to see how someone is generally performing without any need to review lists of figures. The fact that there are two central performance factors being measured allows us to drill down and capture/understand reasons for any variation in performance. Once this is understood, the manager can then act.

Using the Boston Matrix in practice

Let's use our two fee-earners mentioned earlier as theoretical examples:

FEE-EARNER 1	Monthly		
	Actual	Budget	Variance
Turnover	8,320	8,190	130
Hours worked	120	134	–14
Return per hour:	69.33	61.12	8.21

FEE-EARNER 2	Monthly		
	Actual	Budget	Variance
Turnover	4,600	5,192	–592
Hours worked	102	81	21
Return per hour:	45.10	64.10	–19.00

Fee-earner 1 had a turnover higher than budget but did fewer hours than required. We can see this fee-earner works efficiently and/or undertakes good margin work but does not undertake enough work. They would therefore be plotted in the top right box: high contribution/low hours. We should encourage this fee-earner to continue working in the same way (makes a $69.33 return an hour compared to a $61.12 budget) but they might be short of work when considering the hour's shortfall. A strategy can then be devised to get the fee-earner into the top left-hand corner of the Boston Matrix. This might involve ensuring they maximize their day and that they get more work (of a similar margin potential) to undertake, as the figures suggest there is capacity.

Fee-earner 2 recorded far more hours than budgeted but the work done was undertaken inefficiently and/or was charged at a rate insufficient to ensure the required profitability, with only $45.10 made per hour worked compared to a requirement of $64.10. Hence this fee-earner will sit in the bottom left box: low contribution/high hours. We can ascertain that fee-earner 2 is working hard but probably overworking files and might need some help in a more efficient way. We also know it might be that they are doing work that is not economical for someone with their cost rate to undertake. Knowing that these are potential issues means work can be drilled into to see the actions leading to this inefficiency. For example, it might be found that the fee-earner is taking too long on a task that could be done in a different way that would increase efficiency. They might not be utilizing the IT system, so training might be required, or they might not be charging out to a client at a rate that allows acceptable profitability.

Summary

Knowing how your fee-earners have performed and the reasons for that performance are critical. The Boston Matrix allows you to identify and act upon the issues that are highlighted and is a powerful tool to raise performance. A recommended Key Performance Indicator (KPI) is to measure the percentage of fee-earners in the top left-hand corner (high contribution/high hours) and to increase that percentage month-on-month. As a law firm manager, you can rest assured that if that KPI increases, your firm's profitability will also increase in a strong correlation.

Chapter 10:
A data scientist's perspective on law firm profitability

By Zev J. Eigen, founder and chief science officer of Syndio Solutions

Introduction

My name is Zev Eigen, and I'm a former (recovering) law professor and current data scientist. I've worked at and with large and small law firms for more than two decades. I've served as in-house counsel for a large entertainment industry studio. I've also been in the trenches with fellow data science and technophilic evangelists trying to preach to law firm leaders that there is money to be made – vast sums of it, in fact – if they would just turn their firms into things that they are not; if they would only listen to reason and completely revamp their compensation structures to properly incentivize innovation; and of course, if they hire data scientists (not more lawyers or firm management specialists), give them a budget and a seat at the table in order to develop and implement firm strategy. See – that's not hard, right?

And so it goes, with firm leadership almost universally and exclusively making small incremental changes within the confines of existing inefficient organizational infrastructures. Big functional changes that question the very existential identity of a "law firm" are few and far between. I call these small changes "faster horses" innovation, as a reference to the famed quote attributed to Henry Ford: "If I had asked people what they wanted, they would have said faster horses." If you ask lawyers and law firm leaders what they need to innovate, they will tell you faster lawyers, better e-discovery, or a better billing system. It's rare that they would suggest artificial intelligence systems to automate the delivery of legal services, or a SaaS (that's "software as a service") model of delivery of automatable output that could render some of the work lawyers are doing and billing for obsolete. The idea of decreasing billable hours is lauded in public in front of clients, and derided in private as the sounding of a death knell for the practice of law.

In the midst of the quasi-technology revolution occurring now – where the rate of innovation lauded at #LegalTech conferences is significantly greater than the actual rate of innovation – some firms are starting to embrace the idea of using data to improve processes. If you're not a lawyer or you haven't worked at a large law firm, your reaction to that statement is undoubtedly: "Of course everyone uses data to improve processes." However, the idea of law firms tracking key performance metrics, analyzing those data and then using the output of that analysis to render strategic decisions at a firm is *huge*. In the anachronistic space of law firm leadership and management, making big decisions based on things outside of one's experience, intuition, subject matter expertise is really foreign.

I will offer two readily available forms of innovation that firms are adopting now. First, I'll describe a "faster horses" form of innovation — a means of improving how the firm functions to deliver existing offerings (billable hours). I'll then describe a "new car" form of innovation that firms are offering to their clients — in the form of a software as a service ("SaaS") solution.

The fastest of fast horses: improving collaboration with relational data

One way in which firms are beginning to figure this out is by leveraging the power of "relational data". Across the way, in the HR tech space, we are experiencing a data scientific revolution. That means that big HR problems are being addressed by new sources of higher quality data, and those data are being cultivated into actionable business intelligence for companies wise enough to incorporate next generation HR Tech into their toolkits. One of the biggest ways in which this revolution is being staged is by the gathering and evaluation of *relational* data. Relational data are measures of how people interact to get work done. By contrast, *attribute* data are measures that describe what people are. Attribute data include measures like educational attainment, tenure on the job, skill sets, etc. Relational data include measures like whether people are connected to each other, how much they rely on each other for information or support, how much they inspire each other, or how well they collaborate with each other. When work consisted of linear hierarchies and reporting, and people spent their whole careers at one job, often in one or two geographic locations in close proximity to the rest of the company, attribute data were more useful. Work doesn't look like that anymore. Not by a long shot. Work is decentralized, global, and there is less reliance on standard hierarchical structures. People work on devices from anywhere and at any time of day. This is especially true for the practice of law. Pressures from clients are ensuring that the trend of decentralization continues. A big part of the data scientific revolution is the realization that relational data are much better suited than attribute data at solving the biggest and most costly HR problems.

	Attribute Data	**Relational Data**
Examples:	Job tenure, educational attainment	Connections among people, how much A collaborates with B
Description:	Identifying statistical comparisons (e.g.: is there a relationship between educational attainment and turn-over?)	Measuring how work gets done, where collaboration is successful or not, and tying that to bottom-line measures of profitability
Unit of Analysis:	Individual	Individual & Groups
Origins:	HRIS, application process, employee surveys	Employee surveys, meta-data derived from email, calendar and IM
USE CASE EFFICACY RATING:		
Selection	B-	N/A
Performance Management	B	A
Collaboration	B	A+
Predicting turnover	B+	A-
Improving Inclusion as part of a Diversity & Inclusion Initiative	B	A+
Change management	B-	A+
Identifying the most influential people at an organization	F	A+

Figure 1: Comparison of attribute and relational data

Another important component of the HR tech revolution we are currently experiencing is the renewed focus and attention being paid to collaboration. There is so much evidence of the direct link between the right kinds of collaboration and objective measures and bottom line profit across a diverse array of organizational contexts. For instance, Professors Brian Uzzi and Jarrett Spiro demonstrated that finding the right kind and amount of collaboration increased the likelihood that a Broadway musical would be profitable.[1] They looked at 45 years'-worth of musicals. Collaboration in the hospitality industry produces happier guests. There is a lot of attention paid recently to the ways in which collaboration at law firms produces greater profit. For instance, Heidi Gardner, a professor at Harvard Law School and former consultant, has written extensively about how law firms should be gathering and analyzing relational data in order to drive profitability. She evaluated billing records from several large firms over time to show the consistent connection between collaboration and success.

Even at hospitals, the doctor-nurse teams that collaborate better are more likely to generate better patient outcomes. In that case, better collaboration could literally mean the difference between life and death. Across all of these diverse organizational settings (creative arts, hospitality, legal services and medical services), humans have to work with other humans to produce some output. It should not be surprising, then, that understanding the interconnectedness among people via relational data analytics is the A+ method for driving bottom line profitability in so many diverse organizational settings.

Even when law firms spend millions of dollars renovating physical spaces to induce "better collaboration," very little is often done to deliberately measure which groups are collaborating better than others. How do you know that the spaces are cultivated collaboration? How do you know that you've assigned work on teams with optimal collaborative potential? How do you know which teams of lawyers require coaching to improve collaboration? Without measuring collaboration and using the data to create the right constellation of groups, employers are missing out on the tremendous cost savings and profit generation potential. There is ample empirical social scientific evidence that would make the value proposition of investing in tools to accurately measure collaboration and to enable the deliberate optimization of teams a "no-brainer".

There are a variety of effective and most efficient methods for gathering, analyzing and reporting relational data at organizations, including a tool developed by the team at Syndio. Survey instruments are available that enable employees to report critical information about how work gets done. Where appropriate or necessary, these platforms take in email and calendar meta-data as a proxy for quantity of digital communication. "Under the hood," a barrage of sophisticated measures are calculated to gauge how well individuals are collaborating and where they are failing to sufficiently collaborate. Those measures are then visualized on easy to understand dashboards. The dashboards are designed to ensure that the

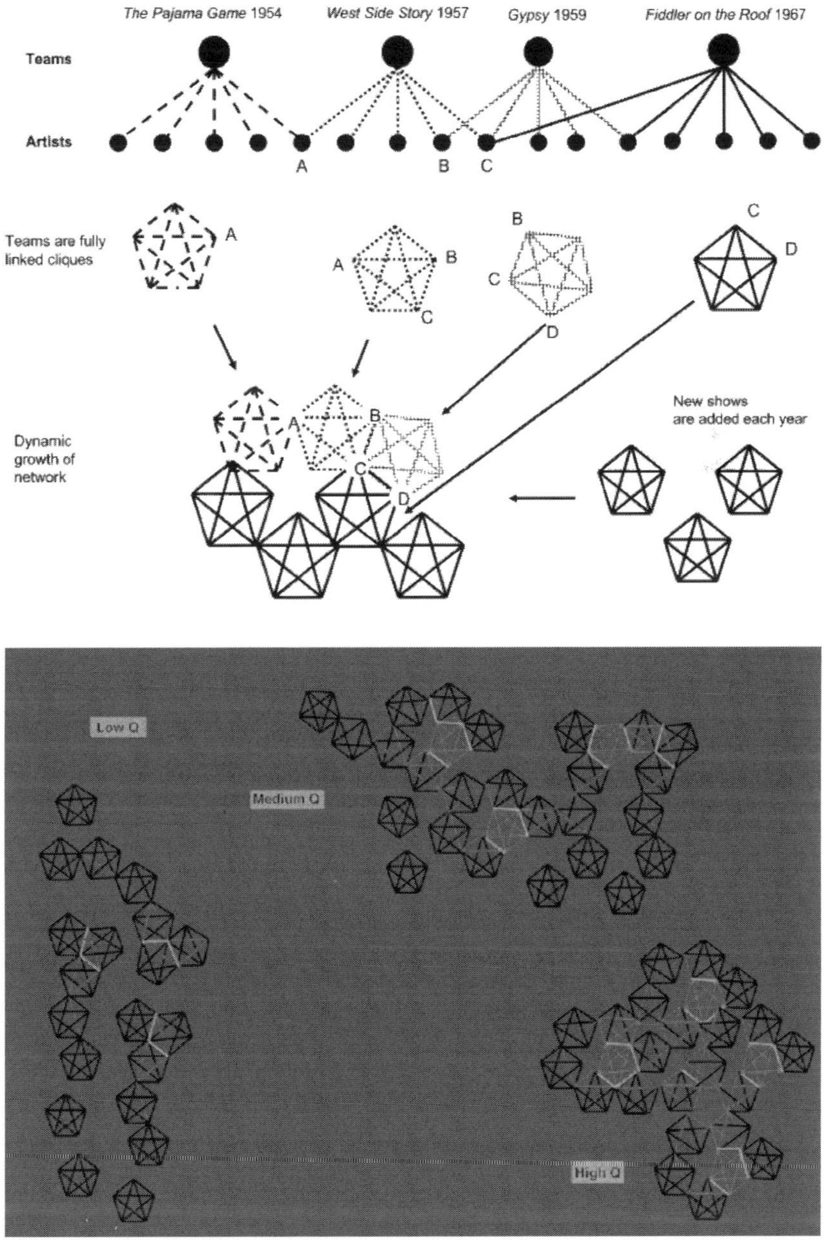

Figure 2: Uzzi and Sprio show that it takes the right quantity and quality of collaboration to produce profitable Broadway musicals

data are transformed into actionable business intelligence. For instance, the dashboard output empowers HR leaders to answer the following critical questions:

1. Which groups are the most cohesive? Which groups are the least cohesive?
2. What is the relationship between collaboration and measurable bottom line profit?
3. Which individuals are suffering from "collaborative overload" (a form of suboptimal over-utilization often associated with highly influential employees feeling burnt out)?

Once the survey instrument is deployed, and the data received analyzed, the dashboard empowers business leaders to address these questions head-on and then implement meaningful change that has an empirically demonstrable impact on bottom-line profitability. Some users employ these data to identify high collaboration and low collaboration groups, forming strategies on how to make the lower performing groups collaborate more. That could mean simply enabling some lesser collaboration individuals to work with the high-collaboration individuals as a way of training them to improve. There are many great ways to use this kind of dashboard information to improve collaboration and reduce collaborative load.

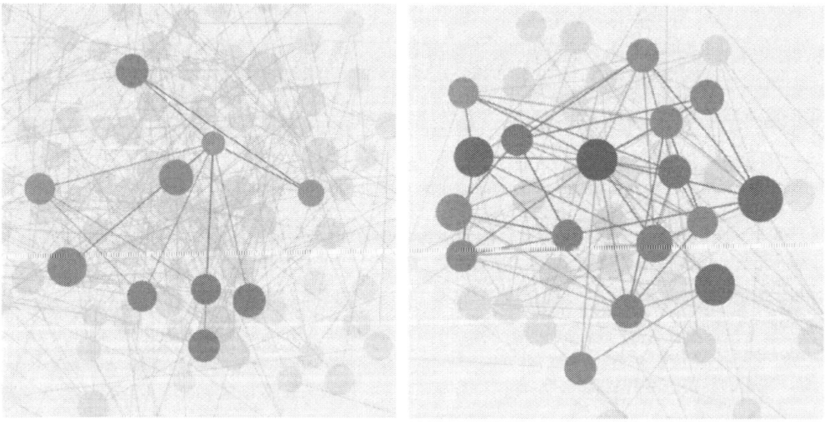

Figure 3: Examples of a low collaboration team and a high collaboration team; the latter was significantly more profitable before intervention and coaching

It is truly the case that, as part of the data science revolution in HR, many better tools are now readily available to employers wise enough to take advantage of them. Relational data scientific platforms, like Syndio's, offer precisely this solution. As a data scientist and someone who has worked very hard for more than two decades to find the right data sources to solve the biggest HR problems, I love watching how quickly and easily these tools enable the capture and maximization of value through measuring collaboration across diverse organizational settings.

The new car: closing the gender pay gap with SaaS

Law firms are just starting to transform the way they offer the services they've traditionally sold to clients. Four factors are pushing and pulling firms towards software as a service ("SaaS") and related alternative technological offerings that are fundamentally better than traditional attorney work. Firstly, the pipeline of talent is drying up as the best of the best opt for business school, entrepreneurship, engineering or other STEM fields instead of law school. This is because the value proposition for attending law school has shifted. It is unlikely the optimum alternative for smart students looking for a grad school opportunity. As the talent pool shrinks, the need for alternatives to labor grows. Secondly, clients are demanding different forms of service offerings, focused on solving business problems. Greater resources are being put into in-house legal teams, reducing the need for costly external counsel for some types of legal work. Clients are loath to pay for work that they know can be automated. Thirdly, increased competition from alternative service providers has firms more wisely mindful of encroachment on their turf. Fourthly, the cohort of firm leaders currently in place are being replaced by the newer cohort of leaders. For the previous group, the model they know and love has always worked, and they are loath to change something proactively. It is like a leader of a yellow taxi cab company being confronted by rising popularity and market share loss due to ride sharing upstarts. They know their model works because of the past, and they don't want to change a thing. Newer leaders see the practice of law as a business first, not a learned profession first. That means closer adherence to profit and loss models, reliance on data for decision making, and a willingness to change incentive structures and offer more innovative optimal things that clients demand.

While there are several ways for firms to offer the "new car" to clients, one that makes a lot of sense is gender pay equity review work. Clients may want legal advice on how to comply with the burgeoning array of federal, state and international laws requiring companies to pay men and women the same for substantially similar work. There are legal issues like, "Which employees should be grouped together for the sake of rendering comparisons?", "What is the proper measure of compensation?" and "What are legally defensible explanatory measures like tenure or educational attainment that may be applied to account for problematic gaps identified?" Aside from those legal questions, the vast majority of the work required is math, data analytics, and diagnostic descriptive statistics and visualizations. The laws do not require a showing of intent. Most of the review process may be handled algorithmically. A software as a service solution is perfect.

Firms may surely opt to build their own version of a SaaS solution; however, this is almost invariably a suboptimal option for three reasons. Firstly, software development is not a one-and-done thing, especially for something like this. There are significant ongoing costs associated with this undertaking. Firms routinely underestimate these costs because they have created other small apps on their websites. They lack the required experience to know how to accurately forecast costs. Conversely, software developers are not experts at forecasting legal costs. Secondly, there are significant expertise required to build a good pay equity analysis tool. Firms don't know what they don't know about building a tool for this purpose. Thirdly, firms are not properly set up to staff around the deployment of SaaS. This requires dedicated customer success, technical support, sales support, deployment experts, and related personnel. In short, the option to build something may seem tempting but, in the long run, it will involve greater than expected expenditure to result in a less than imagined product that requires more care and upkeep than expected.

There is a readily available solution: partner with a vendor which is singularly focused on developing the best available SaaS solution, and pair it with legal services offered to your clients. It is scalable, low-cost, and highly efficient. It offers technology that is in high demand by clients and opportunities to showcase the firm's legitimate commitment to innovation. This is a clear path to optimizing profitability. The firm reduces its cost to bring something of high value to the available pool of clients. It may leverage the technology that's already been developed and is continuously improved upon by world-class data scientists, statisticians and programmers. As such, this is an ideal example of an opportunity to build and deploy innovative technology in a way that is a true win-win. The firm and the client are significantly better off.

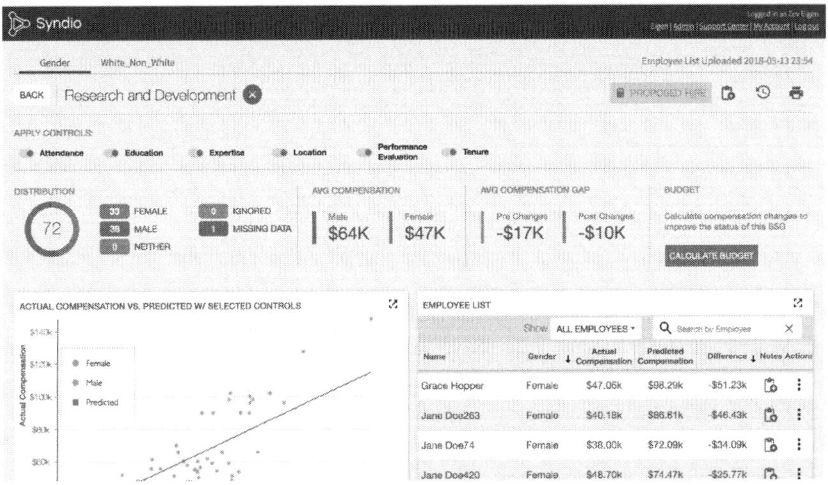

Figure 4: Screenshot from Syndio's Pay Equity Solution

Conclusion

Firms struggle to innovate – a fact which is at the core of the profitability dilemma. Law firms want to get ahead, but they are afraid to be at the front of the pack. They are ill-equipped to properly vet opportunities and often are not properly incentivized. They fall victim of the classic economic problem known as "agency costs," in which what is in the best interest of the agents (lawyers) is not aligned with what is in the best interests of the principal (the firm). For making the firm's functioning more efficient and more profitable (based on empirical evidence) technology that measures collaboration has proven to be highly effective.

There is even a way forward in the faster cars category. Pay equity partnerships with vendors can be accomplished in baby-steps to demonstrate value. For instance, it is easy for a lawyer at a firm to identify several clients and experiment. License with a pay equity SaaS solution and measure the return on investment. Our experience indicates that clients are very pleased and lawyers make significantly more profit than if they had not offered this work or attempted to do it by hand with experts or analysts, or if they tried to handle the work any other way. As the old saying goes, "let the devil take the hindmost." Law firms that swiftly advance to the front of the herd instead of waiting for their competitors to overtake them will reap the spoils of their efforts sooner and more robustly.

Reference

1. http://www.kellogg.northwestern.edu/faculty/uzzi/ftp/uzzi's_research_papers/0900904.pdf

Chapter 11:

Combining newlaw and established law to create profitable business strategies

By Katherine Thomas, consultant and former co-founder and director of Vario for Pinsent Masons

At its most basic level, profitability is a function of the cost of production and the price paid for that production. For longer than most of our careers, in law firms, this has equated to the amount of time a lawyer takes to produce an outcome and the price attached to that time. Profitability was attached to inputs, rather than outputs.

Newlaw has turned this on its head by linking value and profit solely to outputs. Whether it be chatbots using natural language processing to create basic documentation for consumers, or workflow processes that automate 90 percent of contract production, we're seeing a revolution in the way that legal services are provided. With it comes a sea-change in the way clients consume and pay for legal services. Both sides of the equation – the cost of production and the price paid – are changing. This offers huge opportunities for innovative and ambitious firms.

In this chapter, I will explore how established firms can take advantage of just three of these "newlaw" developments to maintain and increase profitability, while delivering better customer value. Now is the time that a law firm can become more than the sum of its parts. It can be more than the price paid for the time its people work. It can spread its risk by making money in new and different ways. These are exciting times.

Client first

We are in a new era for the delivery of legal services. Much legal output does not require a lawyer. In many jurisdictions, deregulation means that legal practices can be owned by non lawyers and legal services can be delivered by organizations that are not law firms. More advanced data analytics and borderless, instant communication have created a transparency to the provision of legal services that simply didn't exist fifteen years ago. The "black box" has been opened. Clients now have choice.

For law firms, this means a hyper-competitive environment where customer needs come first. Customer experience is now essential to survival, let alone profitability. Gone are the days where legal services could be delivered for the convenience of the lawyer. Now the client is front and center. Firms that ignore this do so at their peril.

I raise this point now to emphasize that, whatever innovative strategies you adopt, if they are not rooted in client need, they will fail. If you haven't listened to your client's pressures, pain points and priorities, you will find it near impossible to provide services that address them which are, of course, the foundation of a profitable practice. Beaton Consulting's recent client survey reported that only 15 percent of 154 respondents believed their external firms to be innovative. Could it be that firms are not as innovative as they think, or perhaps that their innovations don't meet client needs? Each and every innovation in legal services delivery presents both an opportunity and a threat to firms. As you read this chapter, therefore, stay on the side of opportunity. Think "client" first.

Blended workforce

Social, technological and economic changes have precipitated a huge shift in the workforce over the recent years. Now law firms are moving away from a large, fixed cost workforce towards a "blended" or "core-plus" model, whereby a hub of employed staff is augmented by contract resources as and when required. By removing some of the fixed cost of labor, firms can work in a more agile and ultimately profitable way. Through deploying this "core-plus" model, the cost of production is reduced because contract labor is only paid for when it is required to do client work. Add to this the overheads saved if those lawyers work remotely, and the figures look even more appealing.

Using contract lawyers has other positive effects that indirectly link to profitability. For example, to do so effectively requires an understanding of when and how those workers are to be engaged. This requires more accurate project management, which has a positive effect on overall efficiency. Or take the way some firms have been liberated by the use of contract lawyers to service hitherto unprofitable new markets. With little or no fixed cost attached to contract lawyers, firms have found they are freer to experiment with new service lines, in a low-risk way. What profitable new services would you launch if you could do so using a low-investment/low-risk pool of contractors?

Clients can experience the benefits of contract lawyers too. In many cases, contractors who work within the firm also fulfil assignments with client in-house teams, enabling clients to manage some of their legal work more cost effectively than sending it to a law firm. Law firms such as Pinsent Masons or DWF, with Vario and DWF Resource respectively, have their own flexible resourcing service to capture value from this trend.

Document automation

A growing number of law firms are automating document production. Technology such as HotDocs can reduce the time spent on creating the first draft of a document by as much as 95 percent. By distilling the document down to a series of and/or components and identifying key pieces of information that are replicated throughout, a basic NDA, will or contract for services can be created in no time.

Some firms choose to use this technology only behind the scenes, to enable their lawyers to do more work in less time. With more time available to focus on client interaction and refining the documentation, lawyers can provide a more responsive, personalized, high-quality service for the same or a lower price, while still maintaining margins. Firms that deploy this approach usually retain their existing charging model and take the opportunity to realize the profit benefits of increased efficiency.

Other firms offer this technology directly to clients. Sensing the desire for “self-service” in straightforward matters to save cost and – competing with newlaw firms such as LawPath and Legal Zoom that are already offering automated documents directly to customers – such firms have decoupled output from lawyers' time, to offer fixed-price, automated document services directly to clients. Allens Accelerate in Australia is one such example. In this case, a fixed price is charged in return for access to the technology to create a customized legal document. The client can then access the firm's lawyers for advice should they require more sophisticated input. Firms using this approach to document automation have spotted the opportunity to diversify the way they make money. They have also identified the potential for fixed-price, automated services to be a conduit to more complex work and a deeper client relationship.

Some clients have deployed document automation directly themselves. Take, for example, the New Zealand Housing Corporation, which recently automated three key construction contracts using LawHawk and HotDocs, realising 75 percent time savings and a predicted $NZ 600,000 p.a. cost saving from this first phase of automation. In this way, document automation does threaten the work that has hitherto been the preserve of law firms. The key here for law firms is to recognize that this is an inevitable part of some clients' journeys and to walk alongside them as they move forward. If your client is automating key legal documents, how can you be part of that development? What help can you offer and how can you adapt to make your services operate seamlessly with the new way of working?

Data analytics

When Clive Humby of UK retailer Tesco said "data is the new oil", he wasn't wrong. Data analytics is the big new kid on the block in legal services, and it's changing not only the way legal services are delivered but also what we consider legal services to be.

Law firms sit on a goldmine of data but rarely, if ever, deploy it for their own or their client's benefit. That's changing now. Through the influence of litigation analytics providers such as Jurimetrics or Premonition and in-house data analytics such as Xakia, in-house counsel and private practice lawyers are waking up to the power of data.

Hélène Russell's chapter on process improvement discussed the value of proper processes to working efficiently to maintain profit health. Data analytics is the mainstay of process improvement. By interrogating the vast amount of data a firm has on its previous cases, deals or projects, firms can identify trends that will help them plan, resource and execute more effectively in the future. Such superior process management leads to more efficiency, greater customer value, and enhanced profitability.

How about monetizing the value of the data your firm already holds? The independent newlaw firm Jurimetrics, for example, analyses statistical data from government, the courts, lawyers and companies to help customers make more informed decisions about their legal affairs. Could your firm provide a similar service in certain areas? If you lack volume of data, could you partner with other firms to aggregate your data appropriately to provide a trends analysis service? If so, how would you price this profitably? Would it exist as a separate service line or would you integrate it into your main service as an enhancement that increases profitability? The data is sitting there: why not use it?

A few law firms have gone a step further than this by employing data analysists to provide a bespoke service to clients. In the UK, DWF LLP is home to a data analytics team that provides data analysis services directly to clients, using their data. This service is provided by DWF Ventures, the firm's innovation arm, in conjunction with DWF Consulting. By way of example, data analysts work within the motor claims team to interrogate client data to enable them to handle their claims more effectively.

Clients are also using data in an increasingly sophisticated way to manage their legal matters and law firms. Xakia is a prominent example.

It helps in-house counsel manage and track matters and, in doing so, analyses the data according to key metrics to produce an easily digestible dashboard. Clients can identify, for example, how long it typically takes for a certain type of matter to be resolved or the relative price certainty delivered by different law firms on similar matters. Remember my reference earlier to the "black box" that has been opened? Here it is – open, in all its glory.

Appropriate fee arrangements

Given that these services operate on a different "cost of production" basis to traditional legal services, how can they be priced for profitability? It is difficult to see how the billable hour can be a suitable pricing mechanism. Sure, some firms may be able to shoe-horn new approaches into the existing structure and make them pay for a while, but now – with the black box well and truly opened – firms will increasingly find it difficult to equate value solely with time.

Now is the time for law firms to re-evaluate what they offer and re-visit what clients value. Firms don't sell expertise. They don't sell their time, or their know-how. Law firms sell solutions. Increasingly, those solutions are tech-enabled, resource-agile and data-driven. The issue might be legal, but the solution combines law, technology, data analysis, process and project management expertise. This is what the law firm of today is selling and it will become increasingly difficult to price profitably on a billable hour basis.

The profitability of the law firm of the future will be based on its ability to identify what clients value (clue: this won't always be the production of documents by human beings) and charge for it in an appropriate way (clue: this won't be by the hour). The profitable firm of the future will make money in a variety of different ways (clue: not only through the direct labor of its employees). It will charge fixed fees for automated solutions, success fees for complex, contingent pieces of work, and prices based on value where the client and the firm share a deep understanding of one another and the matter in hand.

Profitability just got exciting.